From Glory to Glory

by Ken Sumrall
with Robert Paul Lamb

Souls Books · Publishers
St. Simons Island
Georgia 31522

Unless otherwise identified, Scripture quotations are from the King James Version of the Bible.

Library of Congress Number: 80-51487
International Standard Book Number: 0-935452-01-X
First Edition—June 1980
Copyright © 1980 by Kenneth I. Sumrall
Published by Souls Books
All Rights Reserved
Printed in the United States of America

Contents

"But we all, with open face beholding as in a glass the glory of the Lord, are changed into the same image from glory to glory, even as by the Spirit of the Lord."

—II Corinthians 3:18

Foreword

Forewords, prefaces and things printed in the front of books are usually written by famous persons whose names appear on the dust jacket: "Foreword by Famous J. Person." The purpose of this, of course, is to let the prospective reader know the famous person endorses the book and testifies that his friend, the author, will not steal his money, will not steal his wife, and will not lie to the reader.

(That is, unless it is a book like the one written recently by an American author whose opening sentence was: "Everything I write after this sentence is a lie." Oddly, 750,000 supposedly intelligent readers went out and bought that book.)

Do forewords help sell books? I think not. I think not because I am of the opinion that very few people read forewords. Nor do they read prefaces, introductions, prologues and by no means do they read acknowledgements. (That is, unless you are one of those being acknowledged.)

Why then, would a non-famous person like me write a foreword for a book?

I write because I endorse the book. I write because Ken Sumrall is my friend. I also want you to know he will not steal your money, he will not steal your wife, nor will he lie to you. In these days, that's rare. Not only that, but everything in this book is true. That's even more rare.

There are two kinds of bondage for Christians: the bondage of sin or the bondage of traditional religion. Where some of us have had to fight our penchant to sin, Ken's battle has been with traditional religion. His fundamentalist background, his training at Bob Jones University, all make us ask, "Can a man get free in Pensacola?" Yet Ken and his church have gloriously triumphed over traditional religion and have gone ahead to raise the flag for the rest of us to follow.

This is not a "how to" book, in that it does not present pet formulas. In this book you will find stories of failures as well as victories. But as you weep with Ken, and laugh at some of the utterly ridiculous situations he's been through, you'll find God speaking to you, also. For in an expert way, Ken, working with writer Robert Paul Lamb, has woven into each of the episodes of his life, the biblical principles which have brought him through to success. It is these principles, illustrated in the life of a man I deeply love and respect, which will shed light for others struggling in darkness.

Jamie Buckingham
Melbourne, Florida

ONE
Young and Restless

It was raining again. A cold, dreary rain inched out of the northwest pelting the dark woods and fields as it advanced. February always seemed to bring more rain than any other time of the year in southeast Mississippi, and this year, 1947, seemed no different. It was good for the soil, just before spring plowing, but depressing for me.

I watched from a living room window as rain poured off the eaves of the house and ran in exploding rivulets away from the large, frame dwelling. It was a drab day and the rain only served to trap me inside where I least wanted to be.

Most days—even in the biting cold—I spent racing my new Harley-Davidson motorcycle up and down the highways and backroads. On the road, I was free. Being in motion seemed to ease the unsettled feelings I had brought back from Army duty in Europe. I had arrived there shortly after Germany surrendered so I never saw any combat. What I did see was a war-ravaged continent, gutted cities and teeming hordes of hollow-eyed d.p.'s (displaced persons). The whole scene etched an indelible impression on my mind.

I had been discharged only a few weeks when I returned to my parents' rural home outside Ellisville, the small Mississippi town where I grew up. With nothing better to do with my Army "mustering out" pay, I bought a blue and white, chrome-decorated motorcycle.

But I was miserable. Restless. Troubled. At times, I thought I could ride away my frustrations on that "Harley." But I found I couldn't. Women and liquor didn't satisfy either. I had tried plenty of that both in the Army and back home.

Things weren't any better at home than when I left three years before. Daddy was still drinking—just like always. The smell of "Tips," a product to hide the odor of alcohol, was constantly on his breath. Sometimes even in my sleep, I could smell the stuff. And Mother was struggling to keep the family together. Most of the other kids (I was the second oldest of eight) all seemed satisfied. But not me. I lived with the nagging feeling that I belonged somewhere else. I just didn't know where. Life was empty.

"Kenny?"

It was Mother. She had suffered under Daddy's hand, but somehow—calling on strength beyond herself—she had stayed only to suffer even more. Mother loved me. I guess it was only natural since I was the oldest boy and favored her side of the family, the Bynums, with my small frame, black hair and hazel eyes.

She had raised me properly sending me to the Pine Grove Baptist Church. I went every Sunday as a kid to hear the hell-fire and damnation preachers. They made hell sound so real, at times, I'd dream that hell was in our back pasture. I was baptized three times in the Leaf River as a result of such hot preaching.

I had felt "something" in church then. But now, going to church seemed a waste of time. Most of the people I had known were gone. Many had scattered to the cities following the war. Even church left me with a rootless feeling, much like the d.p.'s I'd seen in Europe. At times, I felt like a displaced person.

Mother closed the door behind her lightly. A clap of thunder rolled in the distance. Lightning cracked. "Sounds like we're in for an all day shower," she remarked anxiously. Mother always seemed to get concerned in stormy weather. Whenever a dark cloud appeared in the sky, she would frequently stuff most of the kids underneath a heavy metal bed for protection.

"Yeah, I guess," I mumbled dejectedly.

She sat down on the arm of an easy chair near the window. "Son, what's wrong?" she asked softly. "You seem so jumpy and jittery since you got out of the service."

"I don't know," I said, rubbing one of the window panes to look out. "I just don't know . . ." My voice trailed off.

"Well, son," she said, brushing a sprig of hair from across her forehead, "I don't think things are ever going to be any better here. Your Daddy hasn't changed in the last twenty years. I don't think he's going to start tomorrow."

"Yeah, I know," I agreed, thinking about Daddy's problems, his persistent drinking binges and the numerous business failures that continually handicapped the family. Although he had come from a prosperous, hard-working family, Daddy never unraveled the keys to success. It always seemed to be within his grasp when at the last moment it would slip away. A business reversal always produced a drinking binge. It was a cycle repeated countless times over my youth.

As a youngster, I had tried desperately to please my father, but I never succeeded. By the time I was eight years old, I was plowing in the fields. As the oldest boy, the bulk of the responsibilities fell on me. Daddy would be home only long enough to assign me enough work to keep me busy, and busy I was. Even

on holidays, we worked. The tasks he assigned were unfinishable.
Once in a while, Daddy helped out in the fields. Momentarily
I'd have hope that all the responsiblity for the jobs wasn't going
to be mine. That hope always faded though. "I'll be back in a
little while," he frequently promised, walking off. Then, he'd
come back two days later.

At fourteen, I finally ran away from home for several months.
I was tired of being saddled with such heavy responsibilities for
the family, and equally tired of hoping my hard work was going
to make something good happen around the house. I finished
high school living in the school dormitory and working in a
hosiery mill for my room and board.

Mother was worlds apart from him. Tender and soft-hearted,
she deeply loved her children. Much of the time, he never
seemed to care for anybody but himself. His family was often
treated with the back of his hand.

"I don't know if you remember or not," she recalled, "but
Uncle Jack said if you ever came to Pensacola, he'd get you a
job."

"That's right," I thought to myself. "Uncle Jack Bynum had a
good-paying job with United Gas in Pensacola. Maybe that's
where I should go. I am ready for a change of scenery." I
studied my own thoughts for a while as I watched the rain
running heavily from the roof. A low ground fog was already
creeping across the fields.

"Do you remember, son?" Mother asked again.

"Yeah, I do," I said, turning from the window, "and I think
that may be the place where I ought to go."

Mother nodded her head in agreement.

I walked back into the room where I was sleeping to get a
few of my clothes. "No time like the present to get started with
the move," I told myself. In a few minutes I was back in the
living room zipping up the fur-lined aviator's suit I used in

riding the "Harley."

"Son, where are you going?" Mother asked, surprised at my sudden actions.

"Down to Pensacola," I said, pulling on my leather aviator's cap and hooking the strap under my chin for the ride.

"In the rain?" she responded.

"Yeah."

"But I didn't mean *now* when I mentioned it," she said, almost apologizing for her suggestion. But she knew I was determined. I always had a lot of grit. The rain wouldn't bother me. I was going to leave regardless of what anybody said. That was just me.

I kissed her and walked outside in the downpour. Stuffing the clothes in the saddlebags, I adjusted my goggles over my eyes, fired up the big "74" engine and roared off. Rain splattered the Harley's windshield as I rode off down the dirt road. At times, it stung my face and trickled down the insides of my suit but I didn't care. I was riding and free for a while. Pensacola, a port city in northwest Florida on the Gulf of Mexico, was two hundred miles away.

Sure enough, Uncle Jack and Aunt Mary welcomed me with open arms, and my uncle's promise was still good. Even though there were no jobs available at United Gas, he got me hired in the small appliance department at Gulf Power Company. The Bynum's had plenty of room for me since they had no children. They treated me as if I were their son.

"Things will be better for me here," I told myself, after I bedded down that first night. "I can get rid of those strange feelings I've had." Those feelings gave me the impression something or somebody was pursuing me. Who or what I didn't know.

In no time, I found motorcycle buddies in Pensacola. There was a sudden boom in motorcycling after the war. Indian,

Harley-Davidson and import cycles like Triumph were all popular. Many ex-servicemen were riding them, not to mention the many sailors at the Pensacola Naval Air Station.

Dirt tracks abounded with weekend motorcycle races. Cross-country events were continually held. That's how I spent my weekends, running my "Harley" and drinking with my buddies. All in all, it wasn't a bad life for a twenty-year-old.

A lot of my roughness—typical of the motorcycling crowd—was just outward though. Frequently I just bluffed my way through scrapes. Inside I was soft. And I guess my softness began to show up with my aunt and uncle's Bible reading and prayer time.

They were devout Christians—the praying kind. Each night before bed, Aunt Mary read from the family Bible and then they'd both pray. Somehow they'd always manage to get my name into those prayers.

"And God, thank You for bringing Kenny to our house and bless his life," they prayed night-after-night.

I always knelt with them but I never went so far as to do any praying. My mouth felt wired shut. I don't believe I could have prayed if my life depended on it. Guilt weighed heavily on me. I knew my life wasn't going right. I just didn't know what to do about it.

"One day I'm going to get things straight between me and the Lord," I told myself, after those prayer times. "But now just doesn't seem quite the right time."

Then one unsuspecting Sunday afternoon I came back from the race track. Covered in a thin coating of dirt, grease and sweat, I peeled off my boots at the back door and began scraping their mud-caked bottoms before entering the house. Aunt Mary and Uncle Jack were in the kitchen eating supper.

"Kenny, you hungry?" Aunt Mary asked.

"Sure am," I said.

"I didn't know if you'd be back or not but I went ahead for you," she suggested, motioning to an extra plate she had already set at the table.

"Okay, I'll be in directly but I need a shower before eating. I'm too dirty to sit down at your table now."

"Aw, Kenny," Uncle Jack laughed, a smile lighting his lean face.

I finished my boots and stepped into the kitchen. Aunt Mary's gentle blue eyes met mine as I walked past the table. "Kenny," she began sweetly, reaching out to touch me by the arm, "I was wondering tonight if you'd go to church with us. You've been here over a month now and you haven't been yet. Would you go with us?"

Her question was so innocent, yet inviting, I couldn't seem to resist it. Before I realized what I was saying I heard myself answering, "Well, I guess it won't hurt me much. Sure, I'll go with you."

It was a church service destined to change my life.

Ken Sumrall as a young soldier in Austria, 1946.

Ken sitting on the "Harley," 1947.

TWO
"Ken, When Are You Going to Preach?"

Ed Hardin, a short, balding man in his late thirties, was the pastor at Richards Memorial Methodist Church were my aunt and uncle attended. That night when he started preaching—in a fiery, finger-pointing style—I recognized he believed in his product and I started getting uncomfortable right away.

I just knew Aunt Mary had spoken to him about me. It sounded like he was preaching directly to me and nobody else. "Man, I wish he'd shut up," I thought to myself. "He sounds like he's got a list of my sins right there in front of him."

The church was overflowing with people. There didn't seem to be a vacant seat in the house. Yet nobody else seemed to be reacting as I was. Beads of sweat had popped out on my forehead. The palms of my hands were clammy. My stomach churned.

When he finished preaching, the pastor asked everybody in the audience to close their eyes. "Now anybody who needs prayer for your life," he said, "anybody who's come to the point of needing relief that only God can give, I want you raise your hand. God will hear you tonight and He'll trade you His peace

9

for your unrest."

I knew I needed what that preacher was offering. My heart felt like it would explode as I leaned over the pew in front of me. After a long pause, I lifted my hand must barely above the edge of the pew.

"I see your hand, young man," the pastor said instantly. "I see that hand. You need God tonight. I want you to receive Him."

It seemed like the congregation must have sung fifty stanzas of "Just As I Am" while the pastor appealed for people to come forward. A few did—but I stayed put. I felt glued to my seat.

The service finally ended and I found myself in the church's foyer walking out in a line of people with my aunt and uncle. The pastor was at the head of the line shaking hands. I nervously wondered if he'd recognize me as the person who raised his hand but didn't come forward.

"Pastor, this is our nephew, Kenny Sumrall," Aunt Mary announced, introducing me to the preacher.

He looked at me intently and shook my hand. Still holding my hand in a vise-like grip, he said in a sharp but affectionate voice, "Young man, don't you want to get saved tonight."

Startled at his words, I didn't know what to say. My blank face must have given him an open invitation. "Come with me," he said commandingly.

I didn't know much else to do but tag along behind. He found a Sunday school room where we wouldn't be interrupted and went in. I followed, unsure. Opening a large black Bible, he spread it out on a green, wooden chair. "Let's kneel," he suggested.

Then he began reading about Jesus. As he read—in a gentle, sincere drawl—something happened. The reality of Jesus Christ lifted up from the pages of that Bible. For the first time, I saw Him as a *real* person. He had actually lived on earth and done all those incredible deeds the Bible declared. And above all,

He had died—for me!

Somehow I had heard those things before but I had never applied them to myself. As a kid I had sat in church staring at the back of people's necks thinking "this is good for somebody." But all of a sudden, what he was reading was for me—Ken Sumrall.

Shortly, he stopped reading and asked, "Would you pray?"

"I don't know how to . . . " I said haltingly.

"Do you know how to talk?" he questioned, a slight smile on his face.

"Yes, sir."

"Well, praying is like talking," he explained. "It's just talking to God. You just invite the Lord into your heart. That's all you have to do. Jesus will come in and live with you."

So I just started talking to God, stammering out the words as I did. "Oh, God, I need Your help," I admitted, tears filling up my eyes. "God, You know the things I've been doing. You know the things I did in the Army. I need Your help. I need Your forgiveness. I need Jesus to save me. I can't make it for myself."

As I talked and prayed, a strange sensation came over me. It was something I had never felt before. A gentle peace began filling my body. Somehow it seemed to begin around my heart and float up and down. As it did, I felt all the frustration and restlessness vanishing. All the turmoil I'd brought back from Europe seemed to fade away.

In its place was the person of Jesus. He was totally alive and real to me. And He was in my heart to stay.

I walked out of that room a changed person. I was a new person, in the words of Paul, "a new creature in Christ." Nothing had ever felt so good in all my life. That night—for the first time in years—I slept peacefully.

The next day I promptly went out and bought myself a

Christian Worker's New Testament. All of the words of Jesus were printed in red. I quickly added to that by underlining everything Jesus said. More than anything else, I was interested in Jesus Christ. What He said. How He lived. What He did.

From the start also, I knew my conversion to Christ had put me on a different road than my motorcycle buddies. Those guys went for cold beer, fast bikes and loose women—not exactly Christian staples. I knew I had to make a choice. To do anything less would give me a shallow commitment to the Lord. I chose to sell the motorcycle. That way I could make a clean break.

Cutting my ties with the motorcycle crowd wasn't as difficult as dealing with some of the guys at Gulf Power. That was a daily chore. Since I had smoked cigarettes from the age of twelve, when I quit, it became a signal to most people.

"What's happened to you, Ken?" one of the supervisors, Fred Baker, asked one day as I finished a repair job on a toaster.

"What do you mean?" I asked.

"Well, you don't act like you used to," he responded, taking a drag from a cigarette, the smoke curling under my nose. "You don't ride a motorcycle anymore. You don't talk the way you did. You don't smoke anymore."

"Oh, that," I smiled. "I've given my heart to the Lord."

"You what?" he said.

"I've become a Christian. I've exchanged all that old stuff for a good dose of peace of mind."

The guy, a short man with a tough-bulldog face, thinning black hair and darting eyes, looked at me suspiciously. "You're going to be a preacher, that's why you're so different," he shouted with a laugh. "Old Ken's gonna be a preacher ... that's what."

"No, I'm not going to be a preacher," I answered, my face

growing redder all the time.

But the dye had been cast. Word quickly spread among the guys at Gulf Power. From then on, I was ribbed constantly about becoming a "preacher."

Undeterred I went to church Sunday morning, Sunday evening and Wednesday night. It seemed like the most natural thing in the world for me to do. Aunt Mary and Uncle Jack were elated at the change in me.

That summer, I turned my attention to the young people in the church. Wanda Ruth Till, a thin, wisp of a girl with soft hazel eyes and sandy hair, was one in particular I gave the most attention—although there were others.

"Can I come over and see you sometime?" I asked her one day after church.

"Sure, *we'd* be happy to have you," she answered with a smile.

"Humph," I thought to myself as I walked off. "I don't want to see your family. I'm interested in you."

Despite the slow start, it didn't take long for our friendship to blossom into love and ultimately marriage. Wanda was twenty, a Christian, and had a good job with the state employment agency. She was exactly the kind of girl I wanted to settle down with.

We dated seriously for several months before I gathered enough courage to propose. The night I did we were sitting in here parents' high-ceiling, drafty living room after one of her mother's hearty meals. It was never my style to beat around the bush about something, especially now that my courage was fortified. I just came out and asked her, "Wanda, would you become my wife?"

The question seemed to hang in the air for a moment. Then, she got up from beside me on the couch seemingly in a daze and walked across the room. Sitting down in a chair, she looked back at me.

"Well?" I asked.

A smile creased her face. "Yes, I'll marry you," she said. We met in the center of the room sealing the engagement with a kiss.

Pastor Hardin, who had taken a warm interest in me, married us at the church in October, 1947. Our finances wouldn't allow a honeymoon trip, so we simply went back to the little apartment we'd rented on E Street. The tiny cubicle had a kitchen, a bathroom and a combination living room-bedroom. Our bed came out of the wall. As simple as the place was, it was a little slice of heaven for the newly-married Sumralls.

For three months after we were married, we didn't have a car. New cars were an expensive item after the war. Finally I purchased a '41 Chevrolet for a thousand dollars cash. Incredibly enough, the car had only sold for eight hundred dollars brand new!

The sum total of Christianity for us was attending church regularly and tithing. We did both. And that's the way life ran for about two years. Then one day Pastor Hardin approached us about taking a more active role in church, namely teaching a Bible class.

"What's involved?" I asked cautiously.

"Well, they'd need you for meetings on Friday night and Sunday nights at MYF," he answered.

"That all sound good and I'd love to do it," I assured him, "but Friday night is our movie night. That's the night when we try to relax. I just don't think I can do it."

Pastor Hardin's face reflected genuine disappointment. "Well, I hope you'll reconsider, Ken," he said hopefully. "I think God has great plans in store for you and I wouldn't want to see you miss it."

"Well . . ." I started to say.

"Just promise me one thing," he interrupted.

"What's that?" I quizzed.

"Promise me that you'll think about this some more," he suggested, tugging at my sleeve.

"Okay," I said, feeling pressured. "I'll think about it."

Actually I didn't think about his words until the following week. That's when disaster struck—suddenly. The electrical unions were in a battle with Gulf Power over employee salaries. While that tense struggle was under way, I was caught at the union hall on company time and fired. Even though the union manager assured me I could get re-hired, I was deeply discouraged. My ego bruised.

The following Monday, Wanda was riding a bus downtown to work when she fainted. A doctor's examination revealed two things. She was anemic and pregnant.

"She'll have to quit work," the doctor advised tersely. "Otherwise it could be detrimental to her and the baby's health."

I couldn't believe the turn of events. Both of us were now unemployed!

But that wasn't the end of our troubles. The next day Wanda and I were driving across town to her parents' house. "Ken, isn't that a beautiful place," she observed, pointing to the left as cars whizzed down the boulevard.

"Yeah, it is," I said, looking at the elegant stucco house momentarily.

When I looked back to the road, I knew I was in trouble. Cars were stopped in front of me. I hit the brakes. S-C-R-E-E-E-E-C-H!!! There wasn't enough room to get my car stopped and I plowed into the back of a black Dodge crumpling it up like an accordion. The Dodge, in turn, slammed into a Cadillac. Three cars were demolished including my own.

At first, it seemed as if Wanda and I had only suffered minor cuts and bruises. Then, a closer doctor's examination gave us the real sad news. The baby Wanda was carrying was dead. There seemed to be no end to our troubles.

A few nights later, I went to the church alone. I had borrowed a key from the pastor and let myself in through a side door. Except for a lone light over the altar, the church building was dark and deathly quiet. The place hardly seemed the same as when it was filled with people, but now it mirrored my own feelings—gloomy and depressed.

All of the things that had happened—the two lost jobs, the wrecked car, the baby's death—bore down heavily upon me. As I looked at the life I was leading, it all began adding up. I was only giving lip service to Jesus. I wasn't really being true to Him. On the job, I was making little compromises. I was back to smoking an occasional cigarette and my language had once again gotten salty. Those were hardly attributes of a "new creature in Christ."

I poured the whole mess out to God. "Lord, You know how rotten I am. There's no good thing in me. The only good is in You . . ."

For several hours I stayed at the altar praying. Tears came drenching down my face. Healing and release came through the tears. My heart seemed to overflow with joy and ecstasy. I felt cleansed and purified. Never before had I sensed God's presence so close and so warm.

I had been reading a book entitled *Miracle of Grace,* the biography of "Uncle Buddy" Robinson, a well-known preacher of the early 1920's. It seemed the Methodist Church had a fairly solemn approach to Christianity while somebody like "Uncle Buddy" seemed to enjoy it. I was intrigued by his joyous approach. Somehow I was convinced "Uncle Buddy" was right.

In the book "Uncle Buddy" described an experience of

of entire sanctification which he called "the second blessing." That night when I left the altar, I thought, "Surely, this must be what 'Uncle Buddy' talked about. I must have received the 'second blessing.'"

The experience was so much deeper than my original salvation encounter with Jesus Christ that I knew it was from God. I went home that night with the deepest sense of peace I had ever known.

In spite of the problems we faced I determined to be true to Jesus. Somehow I believed He would take care of the rest, and sure enough, that's the way it happened. Within days, Rufus Matheson, who was a steward at the church, offered me a job selling insurance. I gratefully accepted.

At first, everybody—families included—tried to persuade me to try something else. "You've always been so soft-spoken, Ken," several suggested. "You'll never make it in the insurance business. That's a selling business."

But I was determined to succeed from the start. I had been trained to work hard as a kid back on the farm. I'd apply that same resolve to selling insurance. In Jacksonville while under-going training, I made A's on all the courses. When I returned home, I practiced my sales pitch on Wanda. I'd go outside, knock on the door and attempt to sell the "lady of the house" some insurance.

Although I was soft-spoken and a little timid in talking with people, I resolved to make a success at selling insurance. I disciplined myself to see a certain number of people each week. Never would I allow myself to be under the number I'd set. Every Monday morning, the company held a sales meeting and the manager stood at the chalkboard. "How many people you gonna see this week?" he asked. "How many thousand dollars you gonna write this week?" I always had the highest goals.

I learned a sales pitch—"If I could show you the best savings plan you've ever seen, could you save five dollars a month?" That was the beginning and in no time I had sold those five dollar savings plans all over Pensacola.

It wasn't long before I was making more money in the new job than my wife and I had made jointly. In fact, the job was so successful that we bought a small two-bedroom house on Jackson Street.

For several months we rejoiced in all the goodness we were experiencing. New house. New car. New furniture. The blessings seemed to increase even greater when our first son, Johnny, was born in June, 1950.

In the meantime I had been elected a steward at Richards Memorial Church. Even though I wasn't sure what had happened at the church altar that night, it had propelled me into a new life of service for the Lord. I was involved in as many church-related activities as time would allow. And I continually witnessed to people—even prospective customers—about the Lord, winning many of them to Christ.

But no sooner had I gotten accustomed to our new-found comforts than something began happening to me in church. Every time I attended, I felt an extreme pressure around my heart. It seemed as if something was happening inside of me—something I couldn't control. Somehow I got the incredible notion that God wanted me to preach and I knew I couldn't do anything like that.

"Where would I get a strange idea like that?" I asked myself.

I knew several guys from the church who were going into the ministry. Most of them had held secular jobs, but each of them felt the call of God on their lives. Resigning their jobs, they went off to Bob Jones University where Brother Hardin had trained.

But I knew most of these guys as people with talent and

poise. I was short, timid and soft-spoken. I could barely speak, much less preach. Once I had acted in a church play and the audience couldn't hear me past the third row.

I never said anything to Wanda about what I felt but I made a bold promise to God. "If this is really You speaking to me, Lord, I'm going to ask You to make me the top agent in my insurance company for the year. If that happens, I know You're calling me to preach."

Almost immediately, my name shot to the top in the company's sales reports. I was soon outselling every salesman in the company. I could hardly believe the reports. It seemed as if people were coming out of the woodwork wanting to buy insurance from me.

By the end of 1950, I had become the number one agent for North Florida for the Peninsular Life Insurance Company. Even though two veteran agents had combined their sales in an attempt to keep me from the number one spot, my sales record topped everyone.

Naturally I had forgotten my promise to God. But I quickly found out the Almighty has ways of reminding people of what they promise. I was in the church office one day talking to Winifred Zoble, a heavy-set, gregarious woman who served as the church secretary.

Right in the middle of my pitch about insurance for her son, Winifred suddenly enquired, "Ken, when are you going to preach?"

I hadn't breathed a word to a living soul about that promise. Now—all of a sudden—I remembered the promise I had made to God. "Why did you say that?" I asked, almost in a state of shock.

"I don't know," she responded, totally unaware of what was happening inside of me. "I just felt like saying it."

It was about lunch time and Wanda was expecting me so I

drove straight home. I couldn't think of much else to do. I was shaken. Wanda was in the kitchen getting Johnny's lunch. "I'll be in the bedroom praying a little," I announced, popping my head into the kitchen.

"Fine," she said, "I'll just wait on you before eating."

The back bedroom was quiet and chilly when I closed the door. The wooden floor creaked as I walked to the bedside and knelt. It was January and still cold in Pensacola. The promise I had made God loomed in the back of my mind. Without question, God had answered my request. But now, as if playing a checker game, it seemed my turn to make a move. Based on the answer I'd received, I was supposed to preach. But how? I seemed like such an unlikely candidate for the ministry. Why couldn't I serve God at Richards Memorial?

"Lord, I just don't know how this thing is going to work out," I admitted. "Here it looks like You've called me to preach. I don't know how to do anything like that. I don't even know why You'd call somebody like me. How can I preach?"

For over an hour, I gave the Lord all of my objections. They all made perfectly good sense to me but God seemingly wasn't responding. I couldn't get any relief from this inner feeling. That same pressure to preach the gospel was still within me. Finally I stood up and walked back to the kitchen. Wanda had already put Johnny to bed. She was now cooking over the stove. Steam rose from several boilers as she stirred the contents.

"I've got something to tell you," I announced, taking a seat at the dinette table.

What's that, honey?" she asked.

"It seems like God wants me to preach," my voice quavered. "I don't know how or what it means but it just seems like God wants me to preach."

She smiled as she walked over to me. I put my arms around her waist and held her tightly for a few minutes. "Well, I'm not really surprised," she said, "and if that's what you want to do, I'm ready to go."

"I don't know what it means," I responded. "Nor do I know where we'll be going or what we'll be doing. I just know I've got to obey God. I can't seem to get away from this inner voice to preach."

She rubbed the back of my neck lightly. "You've got to do what the Lord has told you," she observed sweetly, "and I'm with you."

The idea of launching out into the unknown didn't seem to bother Wanda. She was ready to do whatever I felt God was saying. It seemed like God was making a path for us already — kind of like the children of Israel.

Next, I explained to Pastor Hardin what I believed God was saying to me. He took off like a Fourth of July firecracker — sky high with enthusiasm.

"I knew God had something in store for you, Ken," he shouted, pounding me on the back. "We'll just send you off to Bob Jones University but first I want to get you licensed."

Since I had never preached a sermon, Brother Hardin arranged for me to speak on Laymen's Day at another Methodist Church in the community — Ferry Pass. That week, I prayed anxiously, read my Bible continually and listened fervently to all the whiney-voiced radio preachers with their "huh" diction. I thought I had a thirty-minute talk prepared.

When we arrived, Wanda had brought some spirits of ammonia since she was subject to fainting. I was so nervous she loaned me the bottle to sniff but I had practically resorted to chug-a-lugging the stuff before I was introduced. I was as jumpy as a cat in a roomful of rocking chairs.

"Why the Methodist Church needs revival" was my subject and I ripped into it with as much eagerness and zest as I could muster. Preaching as loud as my voice would allow, I banged on the pulpit for a little added emphasis. In ten minutes I was "preached out."

I did not know altar calls weren't in the "order of services" at Ferry Pass. Pastor Hardin had always given them at Richards Memorial. I thought every preacher did. "If you want to get saved or simply get right with God today," I announced freely, "come, get on the altar and talk to Jesus."

Half of the congregation streamed forward. It seemed as if some of the church's most respectable members were getting saved. Even though Ferry Pass's pastor, portly Harry Long, fussed and fumed over my methods—or lack of them—the congregation was clearly stirred.

"I ain't heard preachin' like that since I left Kentucky," a bent, elderly woman, her white hair glinting in the afternoon sun, told me as Wanda and I left the building.

"Thanks," I said, not really knowing if she'd given me a compliment or not.

Somehow I liked that brief taste of preaching. I knew the Bible said God used "the foolishness of preaching" to get people converted. For sure, I had a long way to go as an accomplished preacher but I liked standing behind that pulpit. I had that strange inner feeling again—a feeling that suggested God had something in store for me behind a pulpit. Only time would tell.

THREE
A Methodist Like John Wesley

Through Pastor Hardin's help, arrangements were made for me to enroll at his alma mater, Bob Jones University, for the summer semester, 1951. We sold our house, most of our furniture and paid off the car. It was an exciting adventure we were embarking upon.

When we arrived in Greenville, a city noted for its textile industry in the northwest corner of South Carolina, I had $1500 left over from my home equity so I bought a tiny house in a trailer court. The place had been constructed by a student and patterned after an actual house trailer. Oddly enough, I had to rent the land underneath it.

Just as I had approached the insurance business with determination, I applied that same stick-to-itiveness to college. Even though I had been out of school several years, I made all A's that first semester. In time, I got a knot on the back of my head and some of my hair fell out from studying so hard. I felt I couldn't make a B—that was too low.

Since I held a license from the Methodist Church, I was given what that denomination calls a "charge." It turned out to be a small, rundown mission in a poor section of Greenville. The church already had Ernestine Taylor, a somewhat heavy-set, graying woman, doing social work in the neighborhood but she didn't seem to be making much headway. Few people actually knew she was anywhere around to help them.

My preaching experience was still extremely limited to say the least. I decided to continue preaching in the Ed Hardin tradition. "Hell's hot, heaven's good and salvation's real" was my basic message. Apparently that kind of preaching—even though rooted in the Bible—managed to upset some people.

One afternoon, two somber-faced men dressed in dark suits showed up at the mission. They introduced themselves as "Methodist preachers" but declined the honor of saying a few words from the pulpit. Somehow I got the impression they didn't want to be identified with me.

I preached as usual and several people, mostly folks who lived in the nearby mill village, came forward for salvation. Afterwards, the two men left without saying a word. It wasn't long before my telephone rang with an invitation to visit the district superintendent's office.

My nerves had shifted into overdrive by the time Walter Smut walked out to keep the appointment. He was about thirty minutes late and I had already walked a narrow groove into his office carpet. A tall man with a huge head, jowls, neck and shoulders, Mister Smut tried to be friendly but it seemed a bit forced.

"Young man, we really believe you have potential," he said, adjusting his glasses, "and I just want to help you." He took a seat opposite me. "I just want you to know I'm here to help you."

"Yes, sir," I mumbled, trying to get comfortable.

"But," he said, accenting the word as if to make it stand up end-on-end, "I'm getting some reports that you're preaching things we're not quite sure about."

"What are those?" I asked innocently.

He looked more seriously now. "For example, hell and the second coming of Jesus," he suggested, taking off his glasses and rubbing his heavy eyelids. "We're not sure about those things—so we just don't mention them."

I was puzzled. "What do you preach then?"

"Well, we just tell folks that Christianity is a good way of life," he answered, sounding very pleased with himself for such a pat reply. "We try to keep people on a positive level."

"But don't you feel any responsibility toward these people to preach them the truth?"

"Sure, we do. But we just want to keep it positive. There's so much negative talk going around, you know."

Becoming more alarmed all the time, I asked, "Well, while you're keeping everything on a positive note, do you believe in hell?"

He smiled faintly. "Oh, let me tell you a story—a true story," he said patronizingly. "When I was a young man, Mister Sumrall, they had what they called brush arbor meetings. I went to one of those and a man preached on hell and I was scared. I went home and I was in my bedroom crying. My father came in and asked what I was crying about. I said, 'The preacher preached on hell and I'm scared.' My father put his hand on my head and said, 'Son, if you were God, would you send anybody to hell?' Mister Sumrall, I've never worried about hell ever since. I don't believe God would send anybody to hell."

I couldn't believe my ears. "What are you going to do about the Bible though?" I asked incredulously. "The Bible says hell is for real. Jesus said hell is for real. That seems enough evidence for me."

"Well, uh . . ." he started to say.

"And what about all these people you're preaching to?" I

interrupted. "You're responsible for them. But you aren't giving them what they're supposed to hear."

Mister Smut's face went blank, sagging noticeably. He didn't seem to know any answers to my questions. We had reached an obvious impasse in our conversation.

"I tell you what," he finally suggested. "I believe I'll just let you come before the license committee and explain your case."

I walked out discouraged. The situation looked bad. Within days, a date was set for the committee hearing. I gathered several ministerial students to pray for me. Wanda and I prayed too. I didn't know much else to do.

The committee hearing picked up about where the meeting with Mister Smut ended except this time I faced opposition from a roomful of Methodist preachers instead of just one man. The meeting droned on for several hours while the preachers debated my right to preach what I considered basic Bible truths—heaven, hell, the second coming of Jesus.

In time, my temperature slowly began to boil. I couldn't believe preachers of the gospel would be so insensitive to the Scriptures nor to their responsibilities as men of God. Pulling a copy of the Methodist handbook from my pocket, I slammed it down on the table. Conversation stopped. All heads turned in my direction.

"Men, if I could just get a few words in here," I declared, my voice bouncing off the walls of the stately old meeting room, "here's what John Wesley said."

"John Wesley?" someone mumbled.

"He said anybody who wanted to join the Methodist Society should first flee the wrath to come," I continued, pointing to the book of discipline. "By preaching what I'm preaching, it seems to me I'm more of a Methodist than you fellows are."

Paintings of Jesus and John Wesley—old and fading— decorated the room. "You honor John Wesley with his picture on the wall," I chided, "but you're going against everything he preached. He'd turn over in his grave if he knew what you fellows believed and taught your people."

Dr. Ward Metter, a gray-headed, bespectacled man in his late sixties, was the senior minister present. He kept trying to mediate the situation. "Now son, now son, you don't mean that," he suggested. "You can't mean all this talk."

Finally, I turned to him. "Dr. Metter, I respect your age," I said emphatically. "I know you've been in the ministry a long time. But I don't respect the way you people are handling the flock of God. There's no concern for their eternal destiny. You have a responsibility for that. I don't respect you as a man of God and I sure don't respect your doctrine."

I turned to the other preachers sitting around the long table. Most of them sat in disbelief at my remarks. "In fact, I don't respect any of these men as genuine men of God," I announced.

At that point, the meeting erupted. None of the preachers could believe their ears and all at once everybody was trying to say so.

"When God called me to preach, I didn't hear Him say Methodist," I asserted, pulling my neatly folded license out of a coat pocket. "I refuse to be a Methodist anymore."

"We didn't call for your license," one of the preachers rejoined.

"I know you didn't," I answered heatedly, "but you can have it anyway."

And with that, I walked out.

By the time I had driven home I had calmed down considerably. In fact, I had calmed down to the point where I was low — way low. Wanda was already in bed and asleep when I crawled between the sheets. The streetlight was shining through the window that faced Moore Street, shedding a soft light over the entire room. I tried to sleep but all I could replay was the memories of that painful meeting.

"I've really blown it now," I thought to myself. "When will I ever learn to just keep my mouth shut?" I tossed and turned until Wanda was finally jarred awake.

"Ken, is there something the matter?" she asked softly.

"No, nothing."

"There is too, or you wouldn't be tossing and turning. What is it?"

"I've quit the Methodist Church," I answered.

"Oh, you don't mean that," she said disbelieving.

"Yes I do. I turned in my license."

She was quiet for a few moments. "Well, I know we came up to Greenville in God's will," she said firmly, "and if you've turned in your license, that's got to be in God's will too. Let's just trust God and see what works out. He's brought us this far."

"I guess you're right," I said, after thinking about it.

"Let's pray about it, right now," she suggested, getting out of bed.

I slipped out from under the covers and knelt on the floor beside her. As we prayed, the trouble eased within me and the peace of the Lord returned. Wanda hugged me gently and got back in bed. I lay for a long time thinking about the events. I knew Wanda was right. Even though things didn't look good right now, I believed God had called me. I would have to leave the rest up to Him.

FOUR
Something's Missing

A few days passed and I asked six ministerial students to meet me for a special prayer meeting. The spot was a vacant trailer near our tiny house. The guys stood in a circle as I explained my problem, "I've left the Methodist Church . . . given up my license. I really need prayer for the right direction in my life."

Heads nodded as the students sensed my plight. "We know how you feel, Ken," said Bill Muelle, a ruggedly handsome seminarian from Denver. "You've launched out trusting God and now it looks like a door, you thought was open, is closed."

"Yeah," several of the guys agreed, their voices bouncing around the bare, echoing room.

"Let's pray," suggested Bill.

I led the prayer and then it moved around the circle going from man-to-man. After going around several times, it came my turn again. Suddenly I felt light-hearted. My heart seemed as if it was floating free in my body. The burdens I had faced lifted completely. Joy welled up inside my soul and laughter spilled forth from my mouth.

I felt waves of love flow over me. At first, the laughter came lightly. But the more I laughed the stronger it became. Tears ran down my face as I laughed.

By the time I had stopped laughing, several of the guys had already left. A few were puzzled at what was happening to me.

"No question about it, Ken," Bill said, as we walked out the trailer door, "the Lord did something for you tonight. I never saw anybody enjoying a prayer meeting more than you."

I didn't really understand what was happening either. I simply knew I wanted to serve God and I'd preach when and wherever He made it possible.

The next day I was still filled up with that incredible joy. I felt as if I had to have some place to unload. I got in my little Plymouth coupe and started driving. Soon I found myself in a cotton mill section of Greenville known as Old Bleachery Road. A railroad track paralleled the road. One-room crackerbox mill houses, all painted gunmetal gray and trimmed in white, dotted the landscape.

I pulled off the road and stopped. Light from the afternoon sun crisscrossed the car's hood as it filtered through some nearby shade trees, momentarily reflecting off the silvery hood ornament. A light breeze danced through the leaves.

Leaving the car, I walked off down clay-covered Bleachery Road, talking to God as I went. "Lord, these poor people out here need a place to worship You," I said, not fully understanding my own words. "I'll preach to them if You'll just give me a place. I want to preach for You and I'll do it here."

As I walked along, I noticed a thin, elderly man hobbling on a single crutch out in a garden. From a distance, he appeared to be picking some fall vegetables. I crossed the field to where he was working. "Excuse me, sir," I volunteered, looking into his weather-beaten face, lined and thin, "but are you a Christian?"

The old man looked at me suspiciously and spat a juicy wad

of tobacco juice on the ground. "Naw, I ain't," he replied candidly. "I'm a bootlegger."

I thought it was strange anybody would identify himself as a bootlegger but I learned later that practically everybody on Bleachery Road was involved in moonshine operations. The local sheriff collected a "fee" from the folks who sold the clear-looking but potent brew. For that, the folks on Bleachery Road transacted business untouched by John Law.

"I'm looking to start a church out here," I announced, figuring the old man was a likely candidate for any new work. "Do you know any place around here where I could find a vacant building?"

"Naw, I don't reckon I do," He answered, after giving the question some thought.

But even as he spoke—and spat—I noticed what appeared to be an empty house standing in the distance. It was painted green, had a tin roof and looked to be leaning to one side. "Who owns that house over there with the peeling paint?" I asked, pointing over his collard patch.

"Old man Capps."

"Do you think he'd rent that to me for a church?"

"Maybe," he allowed, nodding his head. "Tell you what," he volunteered, "I'll go ask him." He hobbled up the street and within a few minutes he was back. "Yeah, he'll rent you that place for five dollars a week."

"Well, let's go take a look at it," I suggested. The elderly man, who finally identified himself as Nate Tucker, tagged along beside me as I headed for the battered green building.

Dim rays of sunlight filtered through the filthy windows. Dusty cobwebs drooped loosely between rough overhead beams. Dirt lay in windowsills. The uneven wooden floor sagged badly in spots.

"It's just a little dusty," I said, wiping my hands. "The place looks good otherwise. I think it'll do okay after a clean-up job."

"Guess so," Nate mumbled.

"Do you think he'll let me tear out that partition running down the middle?" I asked. "I need to make one big room out of this place."

"I'll go ask him," he said.

Once again, Nate hobbled off down the street and a short time later he was back. "Yeah, you can tear it out if'n you'll put it back when you leave."

"Sounds simple enough," I replied. "Will you help me?"

He wrinkled up his face, walked to the door and spat again. "I reckon so," he said, "I ain't got much else to do. I might as well help out the Lord's work."

And that was the beginning of my first real pastorate. Tobacco-chewing, bootlegger Nate was destined to become the first man saved in the church. He spent the rest of the afternoon with me helping to rip out the partition.

I had a ready-made assistant pastor in my brother-in-law—tall, thin, James Vanderford, who was also enrolled at Bob Jones. "I know a few Baptist preachers who might donate to our church," Van suggested, as we began making plans to begin services. "I'll try to work out something for benches and song books."

What Van came up with wouldn't have fit at some places but they were right at home in our church. The donations turned out to be ten wooden "pinching" benches (that frequently snagged clothes and flesh) and about fifty worn-out, backless Broadman hymnals.

"We'll need a piano too," I said one day after we had gotten the benches in place. "You have any idea where we can get one?"

Van thought a moment, then snapped his fingers. "There's a store downtown that advertises pianos for five dollars down and a dollar a week," he announced. "Maybe we can get one there."

"Well, the price is definitely in our range," I smiled.

In short order, we did just that. Saturday afternoon before our first service, we had the used piano delivered to the green building on Bleachery Road. We had to make some hasty repairs to the floor after the piano broke through several spots.

"I thought that floor was pretty weak," I told Van surveying the situation. "But we'll just build the floor back. We're going in business for God."

"Right," Van shouted.

We repaired the floor, set the piano in place and got a sign painted announcing services for "The People's Gospel Mission." Our first Sunday service was held in late November, 1951.

I had a few ready members with Wanda, Johnny and our first daughter, Beth, who was born a month earlier. Most of the neighborhood kids stood outside and threw rocks on the tin roof the first Sunday. It was a noisy beginning but the hand of the Lord was on the little church right away. Within a few weeks, Van was asked to begin a mission for Laurel Baptist Church and I was without an assistant and a pianist.

Months passed and word-of-mouth got around about the church. People started coming. Kids and old women—and even a few men, Nate Turner included—began getting saved. Soon the old green building was packed and we needed more room. Further up the street, I found newer quarters in a squat, one-story, concrete block building.

Then, during a successful revival, Clarence Goodnough, a burly, slick-haired, building contractor, came to the Lord. "I want to do something for God," he told me one day. "I'd like to see this church put up a new building and I'd like to do the work."

The people, most of whom were underpaid mill workers, responded eagerly to the plans for a new church building. In time, we were holding services in the white-painted wooden building with the tiny steeple that included an old dinner bell. Most everybody seemed to want a Baptist church so we named the new facility Hilltop Baptist Church.

During the next three years, the church continued attracting new people. People responded to my fervent evangelistic preaching even though at times others left the church because of my "strong" messages.

I preached on hell a lot. I don't know if I was trying to scare people out of hell, or hell out of people. At any rate, hell was one of my *choice* subjects.

And I had a hard concept of God. "He's tough," I repeated often. "He's no Santa Claus." Because of that concept, I never felt God was totally satisfied with me, and if He wasn't satisfied, I couldn't be. Thus, I had to work a little harder in everything I did.

If attendance ever dropped off, I'd just go out in my car house-to-house until I had it filled up. Once I crammed seventeen people in my Plymouth. There were Sundays when I brought at least a third of the people to church.

In many ways I knew the church was succeeding. People were making frequent public confessions of faith in the Lord. I was kept busy with baptisms in the Reedy River.

But I wondered what would happen if I didn't preach as hard or drive around to pick up people in my car. Would the whole church machinery come unglued at the seams? A gnawing feeling began in the pit of my stomach about the church situation. Many times I wondered if what I saw in my church was being repeated in other locations.

In 1954 I accepted a call to a larger congregation, Airport Baptist Church. Actually I was reluctant to leave Hilltop. I felt such a responsibility to those millhands and former bootleggers I'd led to the Lord. But as soon as Bodie Troup, my assistant, was prepared to handle the job, I left.

The new church presented a greater challenge to me. Naturally I was dealing with a different caliber of people. But there was pressure to succeed in a big way at Airport Baptist. I set out to construct a new sanctuary right away. And I was always setting a goal for myself. I was never satisfied with the numbers we were having. If I ever missed a Sunday-oriented goal, I was depressed for several days. The Monday following a bad Sunday came to be known as "Blue Monday."

A prominent family in the church also created pressure for me. Oliver Green was a well-known radio evangelist at the time. His brother, Toy, was a deacon at Airport Baptist. His mother and sister were also members. Somehow I sensed pressure from these people. Although it was never expressed in so many words, I felt I didn't measure up to *their* standard of what a preacher ought to be.

Even though I had given the Airport Baptist pastorate every bit of energy I had, there was still something missing. Yet I wasn't sure if the problem was me, the congregation or the way a Baptist church functions—maybe all three were at fault.

I continually saw people won to the Lord but somehow there was little genuine change in their lives. Once I preached an entire series of messages on the holiness of God. I just knew if I could get people to realize the holiness of God they would want to live right. My own disappointment deepened when that series failed to correct the problem.

"What's the missing ingredient?" I often asked myself.

In time, the pressures began taking a heavy toll with my body. At night, it was so painful to sleep lying down I had to resort to using a chair. Then, I began to feel excruciating pains under my left ribs, chest and back. Since I didn't have a lot of money for expensive doctor's visits, I diagnosed my own case. I figured I had ulcers, heart trouble and a slipped disc.

On Sundays when I preached, the pain became so overwhelming, I put my left hand over the hurting ribs. Toy Green, who seemed to follow me like a shadow, walked up after a service one day. "Brother Ken," he asked, somewhat puzzled, "Why do you hold your ribs when you preach?"

"Because it hurts," I answered flatly.

"Well, we can't have a sick preacher on our hands," he allowed, a look of concern mirrored on his face. "We'll just have to call a deacons' meeting and see what we can do about it."

The deacons' meeting came and they agreed to send me to Baptist Hospital in Winston-Salem, North Carolina. I stayed in the hospital three days being examined and x-rayed from stem to stern. There wasn't a part of my body that hadn't been pinched, poked and probed. Finally I was given an appointment with the chief physician, a tall, spare man with bushy black eyebrows.

His office, located off a busy wing of the hospital, had a clean antiseptic appearance. "Mr. Sumrall, we don't find anything organically wrong with you," he began matter-of-factly, looking over my charts. "But you do appear to be very tense. In fact, some of our doctors thought you were downright hostile. What are you doing down in Greenville that might be making you hostile?"

"Oh, I don't know," I responded mechanically. "Maybe I'm just trying to do too much at one time."

"Our records show you're pastoring a Baptist church and also attend Bob Jones University," he continued. "Are you going to school full or part-time?"

"Full."

"What else are you doing?"

I've got a Saturday job at Western Auto."

He slowly put down the charts and looked across the desk at me. "You mean to tell me you're going to school full-time, pastoring a church which is full-time and you're also working a Saturday job too?"

"Yes, sir."

"How much of a family do you have?"

"Three children." (Stanley, our second son, had been born in March.)

"Mr. Sumrall, it seems to me you're under a great deal of pressure because of all your activities," the doctor said with great assurance. "Your hostility could be a direct result of all the pressure. It's a typical reaction. If this is the case, then whatever is making you hostile, you ought to quit."

Greenville was two hundred-seventy-five miles away and I had plenty of time to think about whatever was making me hostile. By the time I covered that distance, I had decided to make some wholesale changes in my life.

Even though I was in my last semester at Bob Jones University, an ultra-fundamentalist school, I was dismayed over many things happening on campus. Fairly typical was the situation with Oswald J. Smith, a noted preacher, who was asked to leave the school during a conference in which he was the principal speaker. Some two hundred students who didn't agree with the school's actions toward Smith were expelled.

The school had also introduced a loyalty pledge for all prospective graduates. In essence, it said if you graduated from Bob Jones University, you would always be loyal to the school. I didn't feel as if I could sign such a pledge with a clear conscience.

So I made a clean sweep—I quit school, the Saturday job, and the pastorate of Airport Baptist Church.

Surprisingly, the deacon board wouldn't accept my resignation. "No, Brother Ken, what you need is a vacation," Toy Green, who was the chairman, suggested. "If you'll just go off and stay about three weeks, we think you'll be better off."

Toy's suggestion appealed to me even though I wanted to leave the church permanently. So, during the summer of 1955, I took about three week's vacation. I felt refreshed when I returned but it turned out to be short-lived. In no time, the pressure was back. Once again, I saw the lack of genuine commitment on the part of people—no matter how hard I preached or what method I applied. Frustration festered inside of me.

Soon the pain reappeared under my left ribs again. I went back to the deacons. "You know this is a sign I'm getting tense," I explained. "I think I'll just quit preaching awhile and go back to school somewhere else."

But the deacons were adamant again. They didn't feel as if they could release me. Even though I was suffering—emotionally and physically—the church was growing.

"No, Brother Ken, we want you as our pastor," Toy responded, almost sounding like a windup doll. "You just take another vacation. We'll take care of things till you get back."

Once more, I reluctantly accepted the deacons' offer. This time Wanda and I drove back to Mississippi visiting relatives in and around Ellisville. I also stopped off in Hattiesburg to look over William Carey College, named after the famed missionary to India.

A gentle peace descended upon me as I walked around the tree-lined campus. Somehow I felt drawn back to Mississippi. There seemed to be a lure pulling me back to the "piney woods." Like a piece of metal to a powerful magnet, I felt the tug.

Wanda seemed to sense this allurement too. We were agreed. I knew what I had to do.

I returned to Greenville, resigned from the Airport Baptist Church for the third and final time, and moved my family to Hattiesburg. I had no job and very little money. But it seemed as if I was supposed to be there. Once again I was back to basics with the Lord. Without a doubt, He would be my only support in whatever lay ahead—and somehow it felt good in just knowing that.

Ken, left, and James Vanderford outside the People's Gospel Mission, about 1952.

Wanda and Ken Sumrall with babies, Beth and Johnny, outside the second church building in South Carolina.

FIVE

Win 'em and Dip 'em

It was mid-term of the fall semester 1955 at William Carey College when we arrived in Hattiesburg so I couldn't enroll for school. I moved the family into a big, drafty, two-story house with peeling white paint at 600 Tuscen Street. The place had wharf rats in the basement and bats in the attic, but we painted, repaired and called it "home."

Since I had sales experience at Western Auto, I applied for a job there and was hired on the spot. The second day I was in the store the manager introduced me to a tall man wearing a ten gallon hat who was in the process of purchasing a set of new tires.

"Ken, this is Reverend Q.C. Barrett," the manager, Harley Spinks, announced in his high-pitched, vigorous voice. "He's pastor of Green's Creek Baptist Church." Then looking at Barrett, who had broken into a wide grin, he added, "Ken's a preacher too."

Barrett was warm and friendly. "If you're a preacher, I'd like to give you a chance to preach," he volunteered, shaking my hand vigorously. "What kind of preacher are you?"

"Baptist," I answered.

"How about coming out and preaching for me next Sunday night?" he asked. "I'd like to hear you."

"Well, I don't know . . . " I began.

"Are you already preaching somewhere else?" Barrett asked.

"No—not really."

"Then, why don't you come on?"

Actually I wanted a reprieve from preaching for awhile. Barrett was so cordial and friendly I hated to turn him down. "Well, I guess I could make it if you really wanted me to," I finally agreed.

"Yeah, sure I do," Barrett enthused, slapping me on the back.

The following Sunday night the church responded so favorably to my preaching that Barrett invited me back several more times in succession. Word soon spread that a new Baptist preacher was in the area and possibly "available." A pulpit committee from New Hope Baptist Church showed up one night and invited me to preach there. After the first Sunday, the deacons at New Hope offered me a unanimous call as pastor.

"No, I'd rather wait until I preach one more Sunday," I said, preferring to get a better feel for the church and not wanting to rush back into problems I had been so recently freed from.

Ed Lott, a lanky, white-haired, eighty-year-old, who served as the deacons' chairman, reluctantly agreed. "Okay, but we'll just give you another unanimous call next week too."

"Fine," I laughed, "but that'll give me a week to think about the situation."

The following Sunday—a cold, blowy, gray day in December, 1955—I accepted the call. The church, a large white shingle building, was situated in a rural area outside the tiny community of Sumrall. Organized in 1833, it was a country church by just about anybody's standards. On Sundays, pickup trucks outnumbered cars almost two to one.

More than six hundred names were listed on the official church roll although attendance averaged around seventy-five. Hundreds of people had moved off the farm following World War II. That created some loss of attendance. Then, whenever a preacher was "run off," another family or two found a reason to drop out. The latter had happened with increasing frequency over the last ten years.

Since attendance had fallen so drastically, pews had been shoved together in the back. The theory was to force people to seat from the front to the back, not the reverse which was typical of most Baptist congregations. My first move was to change the seating.

"I want those pews pulled apart," I instructed, during a Saturday afternoon work session at the church. "I want all the pews to be available in this place."

"Why's that?" somebody wondered outloud.

"Because we're going to be filling this place up," I snapped. "We're going to have church *here.*"

The four men helping me shrugged their shoulders and exchanged grins among themselves. "Aw, preacher," one of them spoke up, "people have moved off since the war. That's happened over the last ten years."

I looked at the doubting Thomases. "That's no problem," I said confidently. "There's enough people around here to more than fill this church up and that's what I intend to do."

The congregation at New Hope obviously knew it had a preacher who was serious about his calling. I got out my "choice" sermon material and preached on hell Christmas day. I was told later it was the first sermon the church had heard on hell in nine years. Afterwards the altar filled up with people repenting and getting saved. The seating was needed. The church began to fill up.

My snorting, evangelistic style of preaching appealed to the country folks at New Hope. They seemed to thrive on hard preaching and, of course, *that* was my specialty. In short order, I had cranked up an active church program. I visited people continuously in their homes—sometimes as many as fifteen or twenty a day. People frequently came to church simply because I'd paid them a visit.

The church's biggest crowds came on Sunday nights. That was the time when I held "Booster Band." It was an idea I'd borrowed from Ed Hardin. About thirty minutes before the service on Sunday night, I had all the kids sit in the choir loft. We'd sing special songs. The kids would then answer tough Bible questions. And I'd act out Bible stories such as Daniel in the lions' den, David and Goliath, and Haman. The church continually packed out with people—even from other denominations—just to see and hear "Booster Band."

For two years, the church grew. Then, problems began to surface and my new preacher's "honeymoon" ended. The most serious problem came when I installed a rotating system of deacons, similar to most Baptist churches. Uncle Ed, who had been chairman of the deacons for the last forty years, opposed the change.

He was a powerful man in the church and one of the most influential in the whole community. If any faction wanted a new preacher, they'd simply pass the word to Uncle Ed and he'd "run off" the old one. That's the way the change in pastors had been handled for many years.

In August, 1957, I appointed a nominating committee to pick officers for the coming year. In the meantime Wanda's grandmother died and we had to make a hurried trip to Pensacola. When I returned, I called one of the members to check on the committee's work.

Ralph Jones, the committee member, sounded a note

of alarm. "We don't have a nominating committee any more."

"Why not?" I questioned.

"Uncle Ed dismissed it."

My faced blushed hot and red. I thanked Ralph for the information and hung up the phone. "What has happened here when Uncle Ed can dismiss a committee the pastor appoints?" I asked myself. The only way to handle this matter was to face Uncle Ed himself.

"God, You've got to give me wisdom for this situation," I prayed. My prayer seemed to bounce off the ceiling, but I drove out to Uncle Ed's house for the talk anyway. His wife told me he was out in the field pulling corn. I found him "working up a sweat," helped pull a row, then suggested we sit in the shade and talk.

"Uncle Ed, I came by to tell you I won't be your pastor after next Sunday," I announced casually, pulling a blade of grass and twirling it with my fingers.

His wrinkled face, tanned by the hot Mississippi sun to a reddish-yellow hue, had a look of surprise. "Brother Ken, you've only been here about two years and everybody loves you. The church is growing. It's tripled in size. The income's doubled. Why would you be leaving?"

"Because I'm not the pastor here," I said flatly. "You are."

At first, he thought I was joking, but then he recognized I was serious. "Brother Ken, how could I be the pastor?"

"Well, you've taken the authority of a pastor," I answered. "In fact, I think you've been the pastor here a long time. You've just had preachers out here. You haven't had real pastors. I've been called to preach but I want to pastor too. It looks like I can't pastor here so I need to go somewhere else."

"Well, why can't you pastor here?" he asked in disbelief.

"Because you're the pastor."

"Why am I the pastor?"

"You took the authority of the pastor while I was gone," I said firmly. "You got rid of the nominating committee."

"Well, I just didn't think we needed one," he said innocently.

"That's the problem," I answered wryly. "You didn't think we needed one. Anything you don't think we need you're going to get rid of. I can't live with that—so I'm just going to leave."

His leathery face softened. Tears gathered in his eyes and ran down his face. He brushed them away with his work-worn hands. He tried to speak but seem choked up.

I continued talking. "Next Sunday, I'm going to nominate you as the pastor of the church. I'll get the church to vote you in. Then you can go down to Carey College and get a preacher to preach on weekends. Then you can pastor these people. You're doing it anyway, so you might as well be elected."

He bowed his head and rubbed his eyes. There was a long pause. Time stopped briefly. The sparrows in the nearby trees stopped their twittering.

"Brother Ken," he said repentantly, "if you'll forgive me and stay here I won't do that any more."

"Do you really mean that, Uncle Ed?"

"Yes, I do."

"Okay, I'll take your personal word that you'll do exactly that."

True to his word, Uncle Ed never interfered again.

Yet for the next year, I lived with a struggle more real than having to deal with the likes of Uncle Ed. Even though the church was succeeding by most people's standards, I wasn't satisfied. I always seemed to be trying for another goal. One goal reached called for another one to be set. I lived from Sunday to Sunday. Without a goal reached on Sunday, I was depressed for several days following.

At times, I recalled this was the way I felt back in South

Carolina. Was this the way the Christian life was supposed to be all the time? Inside, I felt dry as corn shucks. Something seemed to suggest I lacked genuine power in my life.

The New Hope parsonage, a roomy, green-shingle house, was located on a red clay road about a mile from the church. A pine thicket surrounded the house. Frequently I walked out among the tall oaks, pines, red-leafed black gums and sweet gums watching the squirrels jumping from tree to tree.

Often I thought about the experience I had had while praying with those students at Bob Jones. I recalled the occasion as if I were standing in the vestibule of heaven. Something inside me yearned for that experience again.

"Why couldn't I feel that way again when I prayed?" I asked myself. "Why was that kind of thing so temporary? Would it ever happen again?"

The power of God seemed to continually elude me in the ministry. "God, oh God," I prayed continually walking through the tree-shaded woods, "I need Your power in my life."

Yet, the power of God I'd felt before never really came again. After about three years, I had run out of gas at New Hope. There seemed to be nothing left for me to do there. I had baptized everybody in the church a couple of times. I doubted there was anything left to do but baptize the whole lot of them again. "Win 'em and dip 'em" had been my approach.

A lot of people suggested I belonged in a tent beside the road somewhere—my preaching was just that hot. In time, I began to think maybe some of them were right. Possibly I had a call to evangelism. Maybe that was what was frustrating me.

By the time December 1958 arrived, I was thoroughly restless. The only way I could continue, I thought, was to go into evangelistic work. I called a deacons' meeting and resigned. The deacons were very reluctant to let me go but I prevailed.

The Lord had blessed me greatly at New Hope. In fact, five

people were saved through the last sermon I preached there—but I felt I had to move on.

Some friends, Wally Boone and his wife, Geneva, gave me a house rent-free in Hattiesburg, so we moved back there. In addition to preaching revival meetings throughout Mississippi, I began a radio program on Sundays called "Christ for the South."

But evangelistic work presented a new set of problems right from the start. Wanda and I had four children by this time. Marlene had arrived the year before. Johnny was eight, Beth, seven, and Stanley, three. Each Sunday we traveled to a new town and a different church. The kids had immediate problems adjusting to the continuous changing. Marlene bawled continually.

In a few month's time, I realized I had made a horrible mistake. Although the revival meetings were bringing results, the pressure of a disrupted family was destroying any sense of satisfaction I had with the new ministry.

"For once I should have listened to some deacons," I told myself.

Wanda and I discussed the situation. She too knew we had to make a change—if only to preserve our sanity with the kids. We began praying that God would put me back into a church pastorate.

That prayer was quickly answered when the First Baptist Church of Clara, Mississippi called me as pastor. The sign above the door actually said "church" but that was purely in doubt. The place was more like a funeral home than a church. Without question, it was the deadest church I had ever seen.

It was a welcome relief from the rigors of traveling with four kids, however, and I figured modestly I could bring life to the place with my energies. I had done that at New Hope while getting two college degrees in the process—a bachelor's degree from William Carey College and a master's from the University of Southern Mississippi. I knew it would only be a matter of time before I had everything under control at Clara.

Yet, I was wrong.

I preached hot and heavy for months on end, but no life came to the church. My smoldering sermons on hell couldn't seem to ignite the lethargic crowd. In fact, the only thing that my vigorous labor produced was that all-too-familiar pain, right under my rib cage on the left side.

One cold, rain-soaked Sunday morning I was preaching to the blank-faced, sleeping congregation when the pain started nagging at my side. I stopped abruptly in mid-sentence. People right and left came wide awake looking around to see if they had missed something. The handsome brick sanctuary was quiet, almost like a tomb. Nobody moved. Every eye focused on me.

"Folks, I'm hurting under my left ribs again," I announced tersely, "and that's a sign I'm getting tense."

Most people were now completely following me—a rarity in that church. "Ever since I've been here, I've heard how the holy rollers tore your church up during the Depression," I continued. "You folks don't have any worries. You aren't going to fry—you're freezing!"

The air crackled with intensity as people throughout the building looked around. My voice increased with volume and candor. "If a holy roller came running in this place today shouting, 'Glory! Glory! Glory!', the atmosphere in this church alone would make that person sit down and behave himself."

The congregation seemed to recoil under my words. "I think what God wants me to do is go back to seminary. So I'm giving you my resignation today and I'll be leaving within thirty days."

I prayed briefly, closed my Bible and walked out.

People sat stunned—disbelieving what had just happened.

In a few minutes, several deacons were at my office door. I was still hot, but I listened to their few words. Joe Knight, a plump country barber who gave bowl-shaped haircuts, headed the deacons. He did most of the talking.

"Brother Ken, if you want to go to seminary, that's fine," he assured me. "We'd just like to suggest you let your family stay here while you're gone and we'll take care of everything during the week. You can come back on weekends and preach."

"I'll think it over," I promised without commiting myself.

After discussing and praying over the situation with Wanda, I accepted the deacons' offer. I returned to college, this time enrolling at New Orleans Baptist Theological Seminary. On weekends, I drove back to Clara to be with my family and preach.

"Another degree is exactly what I need," I told myself. "Surely that will take care of this void I constantly feel."

Often on that four hour ride from Clara to New Orleans, I wondered if there wasn't more to the Christian life than what I had. Many times I pondered that thought. I'd attended services in other denominations before and noted a few differences here and there. There were people who seemed to enjoy their faith more than others. Many were rigid and inflexible. Some denominations were only ceremonial in nature.

But there were many things that troubled me—like the Methodist preachers back in Greenville who didn't feel enough responsibility to their people to preach the truth of the Bible. Yet it wasn't just the Methodist. I saw problems in Baptist churches too where the pastor was nothing more than a hireling, hired and fired according to the whims of the congregation.

In the middle of all this, I often asked myself, "Have I missed something? Was there some vital area of Christianity I had yet to encounter? Was the church to operate continually under stress and strain without really experiencing the power of God?"

Countless times I drove across the "piney woods" of Mississippi toward New Orleans wondering about it all. I had no real answers, just plenty of bothersome questions.

*New Hope
Baptist Church
at Sumrall,
Mississippi, 1958.*

*Ken holding
Marlene in front of
First Baptist
Church, Clara,
Mississippi, 1959.*

SIX

Needed: A Pentecostal Revival

Even though I spent the week in New Orleans at seminary, the church in Clara seemed to prosper more from my limited ministry there than when I had been available full-time. My fiery blast at the cold church had produced a miraculous stirring among the people.

In July 1961, three months before I was to graduate from seminary, I received a call to the Boulevard Baptist Church in Pensacola. The new church presented an imposing challenge to me. To date I had pastored only small to medium-sized churches. Now I had an opportunity to lead a thriving church in a large city.

Fear and insecurity dogged my tracks even though I accepted the formidable task. I was following in the wake of a popular pastor, Rowland Jarrard, who still had a strong group of supporters in the church. I knew it would be an uphill struggle . . . and it was.

The church celebrated its fifth anniversary on my first Sunday as pastor. I dived into the job—so typical of me—with as much zest and zeal as I could muster. Committees met regularly and

I chaired each one. Visitation was promoted fervently. Teachers and officers were required to meet once a week on Wednesday nights where I challenged them even further.

I used every promotional gimmick imaginable to increase attendance—most of which worked. By late 1961, attendance had advanced to over 350. The church conducted two worship services each Sunday to seat the crowds.

Nineteen-sixty-two came and with it serious problems. Academic standards for the church's Christian grade school were so low parents were pulling their kids out. I struggled frequently with the school's principal who chose to ignore virtually all of my suggestions. Teachers got angry with me for what they considered "meddling" with the school.

One of the teachers, a bright, red-headed woman, whose temperament matched her hair, was also the church organist. To demonstrate her seething displeasure with me, each Sunday when I stood to preach she quickly turned her folding chair toward the wall. Her actions continually drew the congregation's attention. Some people ended up watching her instead of me.

Then, a more pressing issue surfaced. I learned through the "grapevine" that many of the church's teenagers were going to a dance on Sunday night following the services. The rumor mill reported that the chairman of the board of deacons was actually chaperoning the dance. I was aghast.

The "twist" was a popular dance craze at the time. I was told, "Boulevard has the twistingest teenagers in town."

Reluctantly I called Ray Schaupaugh, the deacon, into my office. A courtly, retired Naval officer, he was an important man to the church but I knew I couldn't allow the situation to continue if all the rumors were true.

"Ray, I've heard some reports that you're having a dance for the young people on Sunday nights," I said. "Is there any truth to that?"

"Yes, sir, we sure are," he answered.

I groaned inwardly. My worst fears realized.

Ray obviously noticed my sunken expression. "Are you against that?" he asked.

"Yes, sir, I sure am."

"Oh," he nodded.

"I don't think it's proper to have that kind of activity—especially not after church. Not to mention the fact, you're the head of the deacons. That makes it look as if the church is approving of the whole thing."

He winced noticeably. "What're you suggesting then?" he questioned.

"Well, as far as I'm concerned, the dance activities must stop. There can't be anymore."

"Well, if that's your feeling, we'll have to follow through," Ray agreed. "But I think we're probably going to have quite a bit of reaction to the situation."

Reaction was right. The next Sunday morning I could hardly see the congregation for the fog in the room. A haze of confusion and anger hung over the church. The teenagers were mad with me. Parents were upset.

I didn't know much else to do but lay out the message, as I had always done, plain and simple. I thought it was wrong and I said so.

People began leaving right away. In a matter of weeks, over a hundred people left to join other churches. At times, I wondered if I had become captain of a sinking ship.

Then, Dr. Gene Williams, a man deeply sensitive to the Lord and a veteran Baptist evangelist, came for a revival in June, 1962. Aided by Jerry Wayne Bernard's soul-stirring singing, Dr. Williams led a revival I had never seen the likes of. He called it, "having confession meetings."

The first night instead of preaching a fervent evangelistic

message, typical of most Baptist revivals, Dr. Williams announced, "I don't think the Lord wants me to preach tonight. I believe He wants us to confess some things."

And with that brief warning, he confessed some minor sins he felt as if he'd committed. "Boy, I feel better now that I've gotten that off my chest," he said freely. "You know sin weighs the heart down. That's why many of us have problems that beset us. Confession is really good for the soul . . . at least that's what the Bible says."

The people sat quietly, not fully understanding where Dr. Williams' approach was leading.

"Now, I have the feeling there are many people out in this audience who have problems like me—things that are weighing them down. Who else wants to get something off their chest tonight?" He looked out over the congregation, a slight smile on his robust face.

At first, people didn't seem to know what to do with Dr. Williams' suggestion. Certainly this wasn't a Baptist approach to revival. Nobody said a word for maybe five or ten minutes. I had never seen the church so quiet and still. It was remarkable. Finally, a bent, elderly women stood up in back confessing a problem she had with another relative.

Then, slowly but steadily, the resistance gave way. People warmed to the idea and began confessing their faults "one to another."

By the time the unusual revival reached the fifth night, Dr. Williams hit paydirt with his confession approach. People began confessing what they had tried to do to *me*. This was clearly Dr. Williams' goal in the first place.

"I've been trying to hurt the pastor," one woman confessed tearfully.

Another woman, heavy-set and graying, announced, "I've talked against Brother Sumrall."

"I've been telling lies about the pastor behind his back," confessed a tall, thin man in a reedy voice.

The front of the church filled up with people crying, repenting and being freed from their sins. Dr. Williams and his confession meetings had brought revival to Boulevard Baptist Church.

Attendance jumped almost immediately. By early 1963, the overflow crowds pushed the church into constructing a new sanctuary to hold 975. A balcony was planned to seat an additional 225.

I continually sought out other Baptist leaders and pastors for successful ideas in pastoring an ever-growing church. I got plenty of advice. It seemed like everyone had a special tactic for getting the necessary results.

Sammy Vaugh was pastor of a large Baptist church in Laurel, Mississippi. According to published reports, he had the most "baptisms" in the state of Mississippi for 1962—a sure sign of success among Baptists. While visiting back home, I drove up to chat with him. A personable, articulate man with a sturdy build, smooth brown hair and immense energy, Sammy was the epitome of an effective Baptist pastor.

"I just wanted to know if the situation is occuring here like it is with me," I began, thinking about the situation I faced at Boulevard.

"How's that?" he asked.

"Well, I'm changing crowds," I admitted frankly. "I have a lot of baptisms every years. In fact, I was second in the area last year. But we don't gain much in overall numbers on Sunday and Wednesday night meetings. We are increasing in number but not in commitment."

"Whew, you hit the nail on the head," he exclaimed. "It's the same way here and really frustrating."

"How about your Sunday night services?" I questioned.

He shook his head. "They're about a third of what they are

on Sunday morning. People will join the church on Sunday morning and won't come back that night. I've noticed people get saved on Sunday morning and won't come back for two weeks. The only thing that keeps them coming on Wednesday nights is the pressure I put on officers and teachers. Otherwise, the Wednesday night service would be a complete flop. But I insist if people are going to teach, they have to be at the Wednesday night meeting."

"You're doing pretty much what I'm going in Pensacola," I said. "I've got ninety-six teachers at Boulevard and they're required to attend Wednesday night. So I'm assured of at least that number coming."

Driving back to Pensacola, I could see Vaugh—even though he was the prototype of a highly successful Baptist pastor— was just as frustrated as I. It seemed life for a Baptist preacher was one of constant pressure shooting for higher and higher goals. Success was never measured in anything but numbers.

And if the numbers ever stopped climbing, a different set of problems unfolded. Once Boulevard's attendance sagged, dropping about twenty-five over several weeks.

"Don't you think you might need a vote of confidence?" one of the deacons suggested testily, after seeing the figures.

I was hurt by such a statement. All suggestions like that did was add more pressure to what I was aleady feeling. Increasingly, I *knew* something was missing. What, I did not know.

Increasingly, I turned to the Bible and other inspirational books looking for a clue. In the first chapter of Acts, I noticed that the believers met continually for prayer after the Lord's ascension. In the second chapter, they were all empowered for service by the Holy Spirit. Strangely, I never noticed what had happened to the disciples after that. They were *transformed*. Peter, for instance, who had denied the Lord three times, preached a sermon thereby causing three thousand to be saved.

As I continually read and researched, I came across the statement of Armin Gesswein, a Los Angeles Lutheran minister, who had shared in the 1937 revival in Norway. He had told a then-unknown evangelist by the name of Billy Graham, "Whenever God is going to do any kind of work, He always begins by prayer."

The rest is pretty much evangelism history. Utilizing prayer bands during his revivals, Billy Graham has become the foremost preacher of the gospel in the world.

Gesswein's statement set me to thinking. In seminary, I had studied the ministries of John Wesley, George Whitefield, Charles L. Finney and Dwight L. Moody. They had all been based on prayer.

That was what we must do at Boulevard Baptist Church. Beginning with just a few men, I started a Saturday night prayer meeting called "The Hour of Power."

For months, the men and I gathered in the church praying for a revival in the lives of the people—something to change their lives for Christ—anything to get them committed to the Lord.

"What we need is an outpouring of the Holy Spirit like with the old time Methodists . . . maybe even a Pentecostal revival," I found myself continually telling the men.

"Yes, amen," chorused the handful of men praying with me.

I don't think any of us knew what a Pentecostal revival was. We just all believed it would help. At least we felt it might. I didn't think I could continue on unless God intervened in some way.

Ken at groundbreaking services at Boulevard Baptist Church, Pensacola, Florida, 1962.

SEVEN

"The Lord Wants to Do Something for this Baptist Preacher..."

The Saturday night prayer meetings had been going for a number of months without any noticeable effect on the church or the life of the people. Then one day, June Gordon, who handled the Church's Sunbeam program with children, came to my office. Normally a bright and cheerful person, she was pale. "Are you sick?" I asked.

"No, sir, I'm scared," she admitted, taking a seat opposite me. "I want to tell you something but I don't know how to tell you. I guess I'm just plain scared."

"Well, just open up and tell me," I encouraged her. "I'm pretty shock proof."

"Well, okay," she agreed, taking a long breath. "I've been baptised in the Holy Ghost and I speak in tongues."

"You do what?" I asked incredulously.

"I've been baptized in the Holy Ghost and I speak in tongues," she repeated.

I shook my head and rubbed my nose. "That's what I thought you said the first time," I responded nervously. "I guess I'm not as shock proof as I thought I was."

"Well, do you have anything else to say?" she questioned.

Remembering my experiences praying at Richards Memorial Church and the time I was baptized in laughter, I shared them with June, who I knew as a sensible person and dedicated church worker. In short, a person not given to emotional extremes.

"I don't speak in tongues and I don't have anything against it," I said in conclusion, "but it's the least thing you can get."

Undismayed by my opinions, she enquired, "May I stay in the church?"

"I guess so if you don't use that little gift you've got," I answered.

"Oh, I don't have the gift of tongues," she said.

"I thought you said you did."

"No, I didn't say that. I said I've been baptized in the Holy Ghost and I speak in tongues."

"Well, whatever it is you have, don't use it around here," I pleaded. "I've got enough problems without any new ones creeping in."

June didn't use her gift in the church but she did begin privately sharing her experience with others. People regularly walked up to me saying, "Guess what's happened to me?" By the glow on their faces, I knew they had received *that* experience too.

In a single week's time, the WMU president, a deacon and his wife, and a young minister in the church had all received. "The 'tongues movement' is spreading through the church," I told myself.

I was furious over the situation. However, at first, I attempted to be diplomatic since the ones receiving were the more stable, faithful members. Thus, I didn't argue against the experience from the pulpit. I simply believed and taught—like any good Baptist—that "tongues" was the least of the gifts and caused too much trouble to be desired.

Yet, when more people in the church began receiving, I felt increasingly threatened. I knew the situation could divide the church if I didn't take charge. Eventually I became more outspoken. As a result, some of the church's most faithful members left for pentecostal churches. All the while, those who stayed at Boulevard, continually deposited full gospel literature around my office.

Voice Magazine was one of those publications. I never bothered looking at it—simply filing it away in the trash can—until one day I saw Billy Graham's photograph on the cover. Alarmed, I couldn't imagine Billy Graham being part of a magazine that promoted the "tongues movement."

Graham's article was entitled, "Something Is Happening." I quickly thumbed to the page and began reading.

"I find all over the country and throughout the world little prayer groups springing up everywhere . . . and people, people that ten years ago would have made fun of you are now engaged in the same type of meetings that you're engaged in, and we believe that there is a move of the Spirit of God . . . It's not in the headlines, but underneath something is happening, and I believe it is of God."

Graham's words struck a responsive chord inside me. "Could this move in my church really be of God?" I asked myself. For many months we had been praying for a fresh move of God's Spirit. "But could this be God's answer?"

But then powerful, negative thoughts quickly overtook my thinking. "This can't be. I've been taught in three colleges and a seminary that these 'happenings' are not for this day. The miracles recorded in the book of Acts were simply to establish the church until the Bible was written and canonized."

I reread Graham's article. He didn't actually *say* he spoke in tongues. In fact, he didn't even mention tongues in the article.

Was he endorsing the "tongues movement?" I wasn't sure.

To better evaluate Graham's statement, I called his Minneapolis office and asked for one of his traveling teams to show a new film at Boulevard. Maybe somebody with this team could help me understand where such an important man of the faith as Billy Graham stood on the issue.

Joe Canzenara, tall, curly-haired man from First Baptist Church in Jacksonville, came as part of the team. Canzenara, a successful businessman, seemed "in touch" with much of Billy Graham's ministry. I decided to talk with him about the famed evangelist.

Calling him into my office, I pulled out the magazine and showed him the article. "Tell me something, Joe," I enquired. "You know a little about Billy Graham. Is he endorsing tongues in this article?"

A smile flashed across his face. "I don't really know, Ken," he said. "I've never heard anyone say who *really* knew his position."

"Oh, I see."

"But let me tell you something—something that happened to me," he said confidently. "This is something I *do* know about."

In short order, Canzenara related to me how he had been an empty church member warming a pew and about ready to throw in the towel with the Christian life. "Then, I was filled with the Holy Spirit in the home of Bertha Madden in Tampa," he explained joyously. "My life has never been the same since. Christ has never been so real. That void—which all kinds of church activities never filled—is now gone."

I understood Canzenara's words. I was well acquainted with the void. It had been part of my life for years. I knew something was missing in my own spiritual experience.

"But could I risk the consequences of a Baptist preacher speaking in tongues?" I asked myself. "That would be ruinous for anybody trying to succeed in the Southern Baptist Convention."

The answer, I decided, was a resounding "no."

Yet, frustration grew inside me. When I had come to Boulevard, I thought maybe I could settle down there for the rest of my life. The place, together with the bustling town of Pensacola, had all the prospects for potential and growth. But by the time New Year's Day 1964 arrived, I was ready to quit. That day I gave the church my resignation.

"I will be leaving in sixty days," I announced to a startled congregation. "I have been accepted by New Orleans Baptist Theological Seminary as a candidate for its doctoral program."

Two days later, I was home working out some of the moving plans with Wanda when the telephone rang. The caller, in a sharp, enthused voice, identified himself as F.E. Ward from Houston, Texas.

"Brother Ken," he said pleasantly, "You don't know me, but someone gave me your name and telephone number. I'm in Pensacola to begin a Full Gospel Businessmen's Chapter and I'd like to have a chat with you."

"Well, you're welcome to come out to the house or I'll meet you sometime at the church," I responded.

"Oh, I don't have any transportation," he explained. "I flew in from Houston and I'm staying at the San Carlos Hotel. Maybe you can come down here."

I didn't give Ward an answer but that afternoon I drove down to the San Carlos Hotel. I'm not sure why I went. People at Boulevard had received *that* gift. I guess I wanted to talk with somebody about it. Ward was from out of town. "Maybe he'll give me some objective answers," I thought.

Knocking on the door, I suddenly found myself confronted with F.E. Ward, who turned out to be an enormous hulk of a man, a wide smile beaming from his broad face. "Come on in, come on in" he shouted, hugging me and pulling me through the door all at once.

I stiffened as he hugged me, having never been hugged by a man before. But there was something very warm about this overweight Texan. He didn't threaten me with his theology and I felt almost comfortable with him.

"Oh, Brother Ken, I'm so glad you could come down here" he said smiling. "God is doing such great things today. Oh, He's doing great things all across the land . . . all across the world. He's baptizing preachers in the Holy Ghost. And He's not partial—He's baptizing Methodists, Presbyterians, Catholics and even a few Baptists! Would you believe that?"

Ward spoke with such genuineness and love I was deeply touched by his description of what God was doing all over the world. I had been taught the age of miracles was past. Healing didn't happen anymore. Yet, here was a man telling me first-hand, he had seen many of these things happen. And God seemed pleased enough to use people like Ward, who believed like a little child.

Tears formed in my eyes. Thinking he might take my tears as a sign of weakness, I reacted defensively. "My eyes water sometimes" I mumbled.

There was an inner tugging in my heart. Something inside me was hungry for what Ward said. I almost felt as if I belonged in those places where the miracles and healings occurred. It seemed like *that* was where God was moving in power.

But at the same time, I was deathly afraid. If I received *that* experience, I knew it would put an end to the ministry I had built. Fourteen years of climbing the Southern Baptist ladder of success would go down the drain.

All at once, I thought of all the important people in my church who were anti-full gospel. The faces of powerful Southern Baptist leaders flashed in my mind. To succeed in the

Southern Baptist Convention, their approval and support was necessary. I knew they'd never recommend somebody who spoke in tongues. They might even consider me mentally unbalanced for such a thought.

I tried to drown that hungry feeling I had. "Well, that's all wonderful about what God's doing," I announced boldly. "But God's moving around here too. I'm going back to seminary in a few weeks to get my doctorate."

Ward thought for a moment, then he responded softly, "Son, God doesn't want you to get more education. He wants you to be baptized in the Holy Ghost and fire."

I had no way of answering this smiling, immense man. Even though he clearly had little education, Ward seemed to be two steps ahead of me with every response. I had three college degrees but I was no match for him. That afternoon when I left his room, I somehow felt as if God had spoken to me. Yet I wasn't sure what to do with what I'd heard.

The next day I received a telephone call from Dan Beasley, a Baptist preacher from West Virginia. "Brother Ken, you don't know me, but your name and phone number were given to me. I'm ministering in a revival in the city. How about coming over?"

"Where are you?" I asked.

"At the Brownsville Assembly of God."

"Assembly of God?" I responded, surprise creeping into my voice. "What are you doing in an Assembly of God Church?"

"Well, brother, let me tell you later. But how about coming over tonight?"

Once again, I found myself going to meet a perfect stranger—all in the space of two days. The Brownsville Assembly of God was packed with several hundred people that night, so I thought I'd just slip in unannounced and take a seat in the back. I honestly didn't want to be recognized.

Instantly, I heard the church's pastor calling out, "I thought I saw Brother Sumrall come in."

People looked around, necks craned to find me. I knew I was on the spot. Politeness dictated I identify myself. My face flushed as I reluctantly slipped my hand into the air.

"Ah, yes," the pastor announced loudly, pointing me out, "Brother Sumrall is pastor of Boulevard Baptist Church in our city."

The congregation applauded warmly. "My trouble grows," I thought. "No self-respecting Baptist should be caught over here."

Beasley, a tall, handsome preacher in his thirties, reminded me of F.E. Ward when he began preaching. "There's something about the warmth and enthusiasm that's the same," I thought to myself. Once again I heard about the moving of the Holy Spirit "all over the world." But this time, it was coming from an ordained Baptist preacher.

Later, Beasley and I drove to a coffee shop to talk. For two hours, he shared with me what God was doing throughout all denominations. "It's the most incredible thing I've ever seen, Ken," he said genuinely.

I had no way of disputing him. And again, almost before I could stop them, tears came to my eyes.

Even though I declined future invitations to attend the revival at Brownsville Assembly, I visited Beasley daily—for two weeks straight—in his motel room. I continually grilled him about *that* experience.

I has seen few preachers with Beasley's joy. He seemed to bubble over with happiness and enthusiasm. "And I didn't have this before the Baptism in the Holy Spirit," he assured me. "I was powerless and ineffective before. My ministry stumbled from one problem to the next."

"If the experience made that much difference in a preacher's ministry, maybe I ought to ask for it," I reluctantly decided. For weeks, I had heard that message. Maybe now was the time to find out.

Beasley was lying on one of the beds praying in tongues. The motel room was quiet. I figured now was as good a time as any to ask. Spreading my handkerchief over my face, I announced quietly, "Alright Lord, if it's for me, give it to me. I'm ready."

That was a giant step for me. I don't know what I expected— thunder or lightning maybe—but neither of those occurred. In fact, nothing happened. I lay on the other bed for ten or fifteen minutes waiting for something—anything.

Finally, I took the handkerchief off. All I felt was defeat and embarrassment. "This thing isn't for me, Dan," I said, getting up to return home.

"Aw, come on brother," he answered confidently, "It's for you too. It's for all of God's people. Just be patient—God has His time for you."

I wasn't convinced but I continued visiting Beasley anyway. He was scheduled to speak at a Full Gospel Businessmen's meeting in Houston on Saturday but since the Brownsville revival was going into a third week he would be returning on Sunday.

"I think God wants you to fly to Houston for that meeting," he announced one day.

"No, I can't do it," I responded negatively. "I can't spare the time and besides that, I don't have the money."

"Aw, Ken, that's no problem," he said.

"It's a problem for me," I rejoined.

"I tell you what," Beasley suggested. "If God provides the money, would you go? That ought to be a clear word for you."

I thought for a moment. "Well, okay, I'll go on that basis— *if* God provides the money," I agreed, never thinking that the Lord would do such a thing.

Nobody had ever sent me money right out of the clear blue before. I didn't think it was possible until the next day. That's when a check arrived in the mail from one of my "tongue speaking" members.

Somehow I felt like Beasley and she had conspired to get me to Houston. Although I felt like I was being manipulated, I went.

When we arrived in Houston on Friday, John Osteen, a live-wire former Baptist preacher, met us at the airport. They dropped me off at Osteen's office and went to record some radio tapes. An extremely likable fellow, Osteen had conveniently left some books on his desk including one of his own entitled *This Awakening Generation.* I skimmed through the book, meditated and prayed—particularly asking God to guard me against heresy. I knew I could be skating on thin, theological ice.

As I was reading the Bible and talking to the Lord, a word— "yahma"—came out of my mouth. I analyzed it for a moment figuring it was something I had learned in seminary. Yet, as I repeated the word, I noticed a warmth circulating through my body.

Just at that instant I was repeating the word, Osteen and Beasley walked through the door. "Praise God, Brother Sumrall!" Osteen shouted, rushing into the room. "You're speaking in tongues."

I froze stiff! My eyes became the size of two fried eggs—me, speaking in tongues, I was horrified.

Osteen and Beasley grabbed me, jerking my hands into the air and saying, "Come on now! Come on now! Just start praising the Lord! Just start praising the Lord! That's all you've got to do."

But I couldn't praise the Lord. I didn't know what I was doing, let alone why I was even in Houston. My mouth was frozen solid—like one of the Great Lakes in the dead of winter, virtually immobile.

After about fifteen minutes, both men recognized the problem and gave up. "I think we ought to go over to Lakewood Church and show Ken around a little," Osteen suggested. "I'd like for him to see what happens when the Holy Ghost builds the church instead of some committee."

Since I knew this was the church Osteen had founded, I was anxious to see the facilities. "Yeah, why don't we go over there," I agreed.

When we drove up, I was stunned. Even though the place had a few bricks on the front, it looked like a large chicken coop—complete with tin roof. I couldn't believe my eyes.

"Well, what'd you expect?" a little voice began to say. "This is what happens to people who get this experience. They all meet in barns. All they ever do is sit around saying hallelujah."

Depression bore down upon me like a heavy cloak. All of a sudden, I felt bone-tired and a little sick to my stomach.

"Brother Sumrall, you look tired," Osteen suggested, ever-cheerful. "We've reserved a room at the Hilton for you. Why don't you go on over there and rest. You'll feel better tomorrow."

"That sounds like a good idea," I said, relieved.

After a hot shower, I went to bed about eight o'clock thinking I'd get a long rest. Three hours later I was still awake. Every time I closed my eyes, I could see tin barns dancing in front of me. I saw my wife's face—wrapped in a big frown. I saw some deacons at Boulevard and they were all unsmiling. And I remembered every nit-wit I had ever met who claimed to speak in tongues.

All night long I slept fitfully, tossing and turning, and dreaming. By morning, I felt as if I hadn't slept at all.

"Praise God! Praise God!" Beasley shouted, dancing into my room about seven o'clock. Then suddenly, he caught a glimpse of my tousled hair, bleary eyes and ashen face. "What in the world is wrong with you?" he asked, a look of surprise on his face.

"Brother, don't tell anybody I've received the Holy Spirit," I lamented, crawling out of the bed. "Last night was the most miserable night of my life. It was terrible."

"Aw, Brother Ken, cheer up," he smiled, patting me on the back. "God's still on His throne. Everything's gonna work out—besides, let's go get some coffee. That'll make you feel better."

Later we went to the Full Gospel meeting and Beasley preached for what seemed like hours. I thought he'd never finish telling his "glory, glory, glory" experiences. Not only that, it seemed like everyone in the meeting was given a chance to speak. As soon as the meeting was finally concluded, I made a beeline for my room, hastily packing my suitcase and telephoning for a taxi.

A few minutes later there was a knock at the door. "Pretty soon to be a cab," I said to myself, opening the door.

But it wasn't a cab driver, it was F.E. Ward!

"Brother Sumrall, God sent me over here to tell you not to go home," he said with great assurance.

I stepped back looking at him seriously. "Well, *if* God sent you to tell me that, come on in," I said, gesturing with a sweep of my hands. "But why in the world would God want me to stay over? I've got to get back to my church."

"Because He wants to do something for you," he suggested confidently, taking a seat near the window.

"Well, I just can't see it," I said, pacing the floor. "I just don't see any further reason for staying here. There's nothing to be accomplished."

Ward, a look of concern on his face, stood and walked over to me, placing his beefy hand on my shoulder. "But, Brother

Sumrall, I honestly don't believe you want to miss hearing from God," he said softly. "I just don't believe you would want to miss that."

"Maybe you're right," I responded, walking to the window and watching the traffic whizz past on a nearby freeway. "Maybe you're right."

Telephoning back to Pensacola, I arranged for a substitute preacher at Boulevard and decided to stay one additional day—but no more. I guess I was *that* desperate for God to do something in my life. I would wait one more day and see.

The next night Ward and I attended the Pasadena Assembly of God in suburban Houston. Even as we walked into the handsome red-brick building, I felt a sense of excitement in the air. Five hundred people were on their feet worshipping and praising God. Hands raised. Voices in unison. I felt that warm sensation dance though my body again.

Pastor Goodwin, a tall, broad-shouldered man, stepped to the microphone saying, "I understand we've got a Southern Baptist preacher here tonight...and he's got the Baptism in the Holy Ghost. I want him to come up and say a word."

The congregation applauded and looked around. "That's you," Ward announced, punching me in the ribs.

"Huh? What?"

"Just go on and give a word for the Lord," Ward instructed, pushing me out of my seat and into the aisle.

I wandered to the platform nervous and slightly bewildered as the congregation applauded and raised their hands. "Folks, the preacher said I've got the Holy Ghost but I don't know whether I do or not," I admitted wearily, looking out over the crowd. "My wife didn't want me to come out here in the first place. My deacons don't know I'm here. Besides that, I've got low blood pressure and I want ya'll to pray for me."

Obviously they had six men programmed for statements

such as "Ya'll pray for me." That's the number of guys who jumped out of the audience and ran to the platform. They began laying hands all over me shouting, "Praise the Lord! Thank You, Jesus!"

One of the men had me around the coat lapels shouting in my face, "Yeow! Glory to God! You're healed! You're healed! I know you're healed! I felt it when he got it! Glory to God!"

They finally released me and I returned—embarrassed and humiliated—to my seat. Secretly I was looking for some way to get out of the service. I *knew* I shouldn't be in a place like this. I was a respectable Baptist preacher with a successful ministry. How did I get roped into all this?

The congregation started into song again. This time, a beautiful, uplifting number called "Sweet Jesus." The roof of the building seemed to lift up as they sang the refrain over and over—"Sweet Jesus, Sweet Jesus, what a wonder You are..."

Then Ward nudged me in the ribs again. "What now?" I thought.

"Get ready," he said.

"For what?"

"Brother, God is going to do something for you tonight," he said positively.

"I thought He'd already done it," I shot back.

"Not yet."

And with that, Ward began waving his over-sized hands high in the air. "Here we go again," I said to myself.

The singing stopped and Pastor Goodwin asked, "What is it, Brother Ward?"

"The Lord wants to do something for this Baptist preacher," Ward announced boldly, pointing to me.

"Well, Brother Ward, come take the service," the pastor replied.

Ward wobbled off to the platform as a hush fell over the

crowd. He looked back at me. "Brother Sumrall, God wants you to get up and walk around the altar," he instructed.

It seemed as if I had five hundred pair of eyes trained on me. I didn't see anyway I could get out of following Ward's instructions. So—I got up and proceeded walking mechanically around the altar.

"Lift up your hands," Ward shouted as I passed in front of the pulpit. I got my hands up about half-way and then hurriedly started back toward my seat.

"No! No! Don't go sit down," he said, calling me back to the front. "God has something special for you. Come up to the platform."

I walked up on the platform as Ward continued giving instructions. "Now everybody get quiet because God is going to say a word to Brother Sumrall."

A holy stillness moved over the building. Everyone waited.

Then, a woman—tall, slender and silver-haired—rose from her seat and started toward me. Immediately I felt myself stiffen. Then I looked at her face. It was glowing, almost angelic. I had never seen such beauty. It suddenly occurred to me, "That's how Stephen's face must have looked" (Acts 6:15). All at once I felt apprehension leave and I relaxed.

Reaching me, she extended her hands and I took them. Then, she began speaking in tongues as she gently pulled me across the platform and back again—like a divine choreography. She ended the message with "Ha-ha! Ha-ha!"

The laughter puzzled me. "If that's God speaking, He must be tickled about something," I thought to myself.

Before I knew it, Pastor Goodwin had taken my hands and was walking in the same pattern as did the woman. "Thus saith the Spirit of the Lord," he declared. "My son, I want to walk with you. And I want you to walk with Me. And as we go walking along together, we will walk all over the land. And you will speak My Word. And as you speak, My Spirit will be upon you as the oil that ran down over Aaron's beard to the skirts of his garments, so shall My Spirit be upon you. And as you speak, many people will come to know Me. A lot of them will come weeping but a host of others will come laughing, saying 'ha-ha, ha-ha'."

Suddenly I was free!

All the old fears, the insecurities were gone. Hearing the Word of the Lord spoken directly to me broke the yoke of bondage. All the inner turmoil and conflict fell away.

My hands shot up and I was praising God and speaking in tongues all at once. It was as if some button had been pushed inside me. Five hundred people joined me. We were all praising God together. For the first time that night, I felt a part of the group. It didn't matter anymore if I were a Baptist or not.

All that mattered was God was going to walk with me. His Spirit was going to be upon me. And I was going to minister His Word to the whole world. I had been set free!

EIGHT
A Church Named Liberty

The next day I flew back to Pensacola hardly needing an airplane for transportation. "Well, did you get what you went for?" Wanda asked, as we walked through the busy airport terminal.

"Hallelujah," I responded, a wide smile punctuating my answer.

She stopped dead in her tracks, people walking around her. A look of sadness flickered across her pretty face followed by hot tears.

That didn't seem like calm, unemotional Wanda. She had always been so level-headed especially every "Blue Monday" when I sat at the breakfast table resigning the church after a bad Sunday. On those days, she always said, "Darling, you're just tired. Things will look better tomorrow."

Now it seemed like my turn to cheer her up. "Honey, what are you crying about?" I questioned, taking her trembling hand.

"What are we going to do with all our bills when you get fired?" she asked through the tears.

I gave her an indulgent smile. "Honey, I'm not going to get fired," I answered. "The deacons will accept this."

"No, they won't," she said firmly, shaking her head. "You'll get fired."

Little did I know *that* was Wanda's first prophecy.

Yet, the remainder of the week I spent trying to convince her that God had everything under control. Realistically, I knew we might wind up out in the street, but I reasoned if we did the Lord would have to go too. Afterall, He'd gotten me into this situation.

Word quickly spread what had happened to me in Houston. Pastor Carl Arnold telephoned asking me to give my *new* testimony at Brownsville Assembly on Thursday night. I readily agreed. Part of the congregation that night included four of my deacons. How they got word of the meeting, I'll never know...the grapevine, I guess.

The next day the chairman of the deacons knocked on my office door at the church. "Come in," I said, looking up from my desk.

He barely opened the door but gave me a hastily printed notice from the hallway. "Deacons' meeting tonight, seven-thirty," he announced tersely, and then hurriedly closed the door.

"Hmmmm," I pondered. It looked as if problems were ahead.

The deacons' meeting was well-attended that night. Twelve deacons, the Associate Pastor, the Treasurer and myself all gathered around the long table. Except for myself, it was a somber-faced gathering. My heart pounded a little faster than usual.

I wondered what I'd say to the men when asked. I didn't have anything planned. How was I going to explain the situation in terms they would understand? I wasn't sure.

"Brother Sumrall," began Marshall Black, the short, heavy-set chairman, a worried look creasing his face. "I've got a copy of the church bulletin that says your Sunday night topic will be 'How I Received the Baptism in the Holy Ghost'."

Tension in the room mounted. Chairs shuffled uneasily.

Black cleared his throat. "Tell us," he said anxiously, "what in the world has happened to you?"

Heads nodded all around the table. It seemed everybody wanted to know as I looked at the men's faces.

A deep, settling peace descended upon me as I stood. "Brethren, some of you have been here with us when we cried out to God on Saturday night—'Oh, God, we're hungry. We want more. We want the Holy Ghost power'—That's what this is all about. It's about the power of the Holy Spirit. The force that has been virtually ignored since the first century."

"Well, that's probably true," one of the deacons mumbled.

Then, Jim Moore, a thin, balding man spoke up. "Brother Sumrall, I don't doubt you've got something—something that is real. But if you mention this, it will tear this church to pieces."

"That's right," chorused several deacons.

"And we owe all kinds of money on these buildings," Moore continued plaintively, his deep-set brown eyes reflecting concern. "How are we going to pay these debts here if this church tears up? How, I ask you?"

I understood the dilemma these men faced. I ought to know. I had taught them to believe *that* way—that "tongues" was divisive and the least of the gifts. They were sincere, God-fearing men for the most part, but they could not rise above their tradition. My *new* experience was not Baptist and thus they believed it had no place in a Baptist church. It threatened the church's very existence.

It was evident there was only one solution left. I made it easy for them by going ahead to say so.

"Well, men why don't you just let me slip out of here," I offered. "I have already resigned from the church anyway.

Even though the sixty days isn't out, I can leave. You can explain what has happened in whatever way you choose."

The deacons readily agreed. That was the easiest way.

That night I walked out of the church into the cold, windy air as happy as a school boy just released for the summer holidays. As I did, I remembered when that building had been put up. I had watched all the steel and bricks go into place. That building was a part of me. Yet, in one moment, it had become a part of my past. I was an outsider now.

I realized what had just happened. I had left a generous retirement program, a fourteen-year reputation in the Southern Baptist Convention and a lot of friends. Yet God was moving on and I knew I had to follow wherever He led.

Instead of heading straight home, I drove to the Brownsville Assembly of God where that same revival meeting with Dan Beasley was still in progress. I kinda dreaded facing Wanda. Her worst fears were now realized—we were going to be put out.

All week long she had seemed anxious and tense. Since returning to her hometown of Pensacola, we had settled into a secure pastorate. Now all of that was being changed. Like most women would have done, she wrestled with the insecurity of the situation. Thus I feared what had happened might upset her even more.

It was almost midnight when I arrived home. The house was quiet. The kids were in bed. A lone light was lit in the den. I stood for a few moments looking at Wanda, crumpled up in a robe, napping on the couch. An open Bible lay on the coffee table.

I picked it up and looked at what she had been reading. She had underlined the words of Proverbs 3:5,6. "Trust in the Lord with all thine heart; and lean not unto thine own understanding. In all thy ways acknowledge him, and he shall direct thy paths."

"Words for the Sumrall family," I thought to myself.

I reached down and gave Wanda a light kiss on the cheek. She stirred. "I'm home," I announced softly.

"Oh," she responded drowsily, rubbing her eyes. "I think I fell asleep. What time is it?"

"About midnight."

She sat up, making room for me to sit beside her on the sofa. "Well, what happened at the meeting?" she asked.

"We've got a month to live in the pastorium and two weeks' salary," I said, managing a weak smile.

"Well, that's a relief," she said, returning my smile with a broader grin of her own. "I feel better now."

"You mean you're not upset?" I quizzed.

"No, not really. I knew it was coming to this—call it womanly intuition or something. But I feel kinda relieved that it's over."

"Praise the Lord!" I exclaimed.

"Sh-h-h-h-h-h, you'll wake up the kids," she admonished.

"I can't help it," I answered with a grin, taking her hand. "We're taking a great leap into the unknown and I'm just excited about the possibilities for what God can do."

She squeezed my hand. "That's interesting," she said. "I was just reading in the Bible tonight and it seemed as if I saw so many verses where it talked about trusting God for everything you need. I know we've done it before and we can do it again. You know, I'm willing."

"Well, the Sumralls will have a good chance to do just that," I agreed. "I don't really know where God is leading but it sure looks like we're on our way."

The next morning, Wanda and I attended a Full Gospel Businessmen's Meeting at the San Carlos Hotel in downtown Pensacola. We listened to the speaker's testimony and then people were invited forward to receive the Baptism with the Holy Spirit. I went up to assist in praying for people.

Amidst all the activity, I looked back at Wanda still seated at our table. She had not yet received the baptism. I knew it was a *must* for whatever lay ahead. Walking back to where she was seated, I said, "I don't want to insist that you go forward but . . . " and I paused.

Without a moment's hesitation, she stood up and went with me. Henry Alloway, a soft-spoken, Methodist pastor from Texas, saw us coming forward and walked over. "Can I take you back to a prayer room with several of these ladies to pray over you?" he asked Wanda, a smile lighting his sensitive face.

"Yes, I'd like that," Wanda answered, nodding her head.

Pastor Alloway, the two women and Wanda were gone for almost two hours. The room was practically empty of people when they returned. I didn't have to ask if Wanda had received the baptism. Her face told the whole story. It was bright and shining, like a noonday sun.

"I can't remember actually speaking in tongues," Wanda said beaming. "After they prayed for me, I fainted or something . . . that's all I remember."

"That's okay, Wanda," Pastor Alloway spoke up. "I was there in the company of two witnesses and you did! Praise the Lord!"

"Praise God," I agreed.

Our black, metal mailbox was slightly ajar when we pulled into the driveway. Its tiny red flag was also raised. "Looks like the mailman has already come by," Wanda suggested. "Let me out and I'll get the mail. I've already felt something might be here."

I stopped the car while Wanda walked the short distance to the box. She retrieved the bundle of mail and sifted through it as she walked.

"Ken, Ken," she shouted, running up the driveway to where I had parked the car and was unloading some boxes.

I dropped the boxes anxiously. "What's up?"

"Look what the Lord has given us!" she called out, a yellow piece of paper fluttering in her hand.

"Why, it's a check for two hundred dollars," I said, taking the envelope. "Wow! I can't believe it."

"It's just like God's placing His seal of approval on all that changes in our lives," Wanda suggested, her sandy hair glinting in the afternoon sun.

I looked at the check almost disbelieving as I read the figures again. "So much is happening," I mumbled, walking arm in arm into the house. "From Sunday through today, we've both received the baptism. Now this check comes to help us along. Sometimes I think I need to pinch myself to see if I'm dreaming."

I wasn't dreaming though and I wasn't worried either—even though I still had problems. The next two weeks I spent trying to locate another house for the family. Time was running out for us to vacate the pastorium and I wasn't having any success. I could just see all our furniture being unceremoniously dumped on the sidewalk at the end of the two weeks.

The revival meetings—which eventually ran six weeks long— were still underway at Brownsville Assembly. Several preachers had been involved in the revival—Beasley, Alloway and Bob Buess, who was preaching the Saturday morning I attended.

I sat through the service half-listening, mostly thinking about our desperate need for a house. At the close of the service, I went forward for prayer. Buess was praying for people at the altar when he approached me. A rough-talking, coarse man, he asked curtly, "What'd you want?"

"I need a house," I said softly, "and I need it fairly soon. I've got to move out of a pastorium where I'm staying in just a couple of days."

He looked at me for a moment. A strange expression crossed

his face. Then, he walked to the other side of the platform. Before I could think twice, he was charging across the front of the church running straight at me. He banged into me at full-speed shouting, "Give 'em a house, Lord."

I landed in a heap on the floor. "Well, I've never been prayed for like that before," I said, picking myself off the floor, "but if it works . . . who knows?"

Sure enough, Buess' unorthodox prayer worked!

We had been looking at houses for nearly two weeks straight, but none of them suited us, a family with four growing children. That afternoon, Wanda was looking through the newspaper want ads. "How about this?" she asked. "Four bedroom split-level with basement."

"Where's it located?"

"On Chadwick. I think that's on the east side of town."

"Well, that's the wrong side of town," I answered, "but that house sounds big enough for the family. I like split-level houses anyway."

Wanda went to the telephone and made an appointment later in the day to see the house. When we found the place, we knew it was *exactly* what we wanted—a tree-shaded yard surrounding a roomy, white split-level house. And all I needed for a down payment was two hundred dollars. Now I knew why the Lord had so abundantly supplied that amount when I hadn't even asked. I was beginning to learn how God supplied for His children.

Although my days as a Baptist pastor had ended, I was busy filling invitations to preach among pentecostal and full gospel churches. One of the unique places where I preached was the Springfield Community Church in Panama City, about eighty miles east of Pensacola.

I had never seen a church service quite like the one at Springfield. The place didn't have a choir. An announcement was simply made from the pulpit for "anybody who wanted to sing to come forward." Without another word of encouragement, more than two hundred people then gathered on the platform. They were the choir.

Nobody bothered to lead or direct the singing though. "The Holy Spirit will take care of that," the pastor, a broad-shouldered man in his middle sixties, who looked years younger, told me when I asked.

And sure enough, that's what happened. Under the prompting of the Holy Spirit, one person after another danced out of the choir, led the music for awhile, then danced back in. Yet the music was beautiful, harmonious. No one could doubt it was heavenly orchestrated.

That same night following the music, I was introduced to share my testimony. About half-way through my talk, I felt the Lord urging me to stop.

As I did, a message in tongues came bursting forth from the audience, sounding like machine-gun volleys. The interpretation, just as powerful, came through the pastor. It said, "My son, be not afraid to begin a work in your city. For I have many people there who are hungry for Me. Begin this work in Me, dedicate it to Me, and watch My mighty hand be upon you . . . thus saith God."

The peace of the Lord fell upon me as I heard the words. I knew they were meant for me. It was what God wanted me to hear.

For weeks I had been in a quandary over what direction I should take in the ministry. One pentecostal denomination had let it be known I could pastor churches with them.

Then, there were people in Pensacola urging me to start another church. Some of them—the Kirkpatricks and the Dreadins—had joined pentecostal churches but a few others— the Rhymes, the Hearns and the Roberts—were still at Boulevard.

Again and again, they had suggested starting a church. My answer had always been the same. "We don't need another church in Pensacola. There's already too many."

To some extent, I didn't want to begin another church. I had just been released from that responsibility. For years, I had carried churches on my shoulders. I wasn't enthused about starting another one.

But the prophetic word at Springfield Community Church changed that. It was the direction I needed. I drove back to Pensacola with plans to look for a building. I had confidence this *was* God's direction.

One warm, sun-filled March day, I found myself on Cervantes Street in the Brownsville section of Pensacola. I had already walked into two blank walls that day. Two prospective locations had been rented. But in the twenty-six hundred block of Cervantes, I found a couple of vacant store buildings, one-story, masonry block construction.

The only problem I saw was the location. The next door tenant was an ABC liquor store.

A sign in the window instructed interested parties to apply at the bakery on the corner. I decided to follow through. "Liquor store or not, this may be the place," I mumbled to myself as I entered the bakery.

"Do you know who's renting the store building on the corner?" I asked the burly, sweating man in a soiled white tee-shirt behind the counter.

"Yeah, I am," he answered, sprinkling a pan of donuts with confectionery sugar. "Who wants to know?"

"Well, I do," I volunteered. "How much do you want a month for the building?"

"Two-fifty."

"I'd like to start a church in it," I announced, looking over the case of bakery goodies before me. "I'll give you one-fifty a month."

The man grunted and pulled another cookie sheet out filled with hot morsels. The smell tantalized my nostrils. "You want to start a church in that store building?" he questioned.

"Yeah."

"We've had a little of everything in there—but never a church," he mumbled. "You're not worried about the liquor store on the other side giving you a bad name?"

"Not really."

"Okay, I'll let you have it," he said somewhat reluctantly. "How long you planning to stay?"

"I don't know," I answered, still looking at his cases and thinking lunch was getting late, "maybe six months to a year."

"Okay, let me get my receipt book," he announced wiping his hands on his dirty apron, "and I'll give you a receipt for your money."

"Uh, better hold on there a minute," I said uncomfortably. "I won't be able to give you the money until after our first service."

He arched a bushy eyebrow in my direction and rubbed his tatoo-covered arms. "Oh, really?" he said.

"Yeah, and can I start fixing the place up right away?" I asked.

The guy shook his head and went back to working with his pans. "I guess so," he allowed wearily. "You sure there's nothing else you need?"

"No, I don't guess so," I smiled. "You've done enough."

I quickly telephoned several of the families who had expressed interest in starting a new church. A few of them drove over and we had a prayer meeting in the now-vacant building. Plans were hastily made to decorate the sparse-looking facilities. Someone suggested building a foyer with paneling and drapes to give the all-glass front a more personal touch. The only problem was the cost of paneling—one hundred dollars. I didn't have it and nobody else seemed to either.

The meeting at Brownsville Assembly—believe it or not—was still underway. The Lord had repeatedly touched my life through that revival. The day I found the building on Cervantes, I drove over to Brownsville Assembly again. The church was packed, as usual, but I found a seat beside Gene Adkins, who was pastor of Grace Assembly.

I had no sooner sat down and greeted Gene than the Lord spoke to me. "Give Gene Adkins ten dollars," He instructed.

All I had in my pocket was ten dollars—so I held back—but the Lord continued pressing me to give the money. Finally, I obeyed. "The Lord said to give this to you, Gene," I said quietly, handing him the money.

Gene laughed. "I better get out of here before He tells me to give it to somebody else," he said.

The service concluded and I went down to the altar to pray over the situation I faced with the new facilities. When I finished, a spry, elderly woman tapped me on the shoulder and handed me a roll of bills.

"What's this?" I asked, looking down at the money.

The woman never answered. She simply walked away.

I unrolled the bills and counted five twenty dollar bills. "Praise God!" I shouted. "His supply always equals my need." I knew exactly what the money was for. The next morning I drove to the lumber company and picked up the paneling. When Sunday came, the new foyer was in place at the store building.

Thirty-five people showed up for the first service—March 16, 1964. Among them were: Bob and Patti Roberts, the Kirkpatricks, the Rhymes, the Hearns, the Merritts, Pat Williams and her three children, and Elaine Brown, who had been my secretary at Boulevard. Elaine invited her mother and aunt,

Sister Gibson and Nellie Wooten, who also came.

That night, fifty-one attended.

Several of the men had put together a crude pulpit. Paper-thin plywood was used for the platform decorating the front of the building. The decorator, who had helped with constructing the foyer, also made simulated windows down one side of the building. Metal folding chairs from a local pentecostal church had been loaned for the services.

Within a few weeks, we had one hundred and one in attendance. I was greatly encouraged at the turnout. For the most part, I knew these people were like me—simply hungry for more of God. The Sunday we reached over a hundred I brought an old record album and broke it over the pulpit just like I had done as a Southern Baptist.

Actually the church went several Sundays without a name until I woke up one morning with Liberty Baptist Church on my mind. At first, the name sounded so familiar I thought there was another church by that same name in the Myrtle Grove section of Pensacola. But after driving up and down the streets of Myrtle Grove, I couldn't locate it—if it ever existed.

"It must be the leading of the Lord," I finally decided.

So—the storefront church located next door to the ABC liquor store on Cervantes Street became Liberty *Baptist* Church. Nobody had bothered asking for my Baptist ordination papers back and since most of the folks were ex-Baptists, we kept the name. At that time even the church's structure of government—congregational—was like the Baptists.

In spite of all the carryovers from the past, we were a people who wanted to be free to worship God. I remembered the Apostle Paul's words in 2 Corinthians 3:17, "where the Spirit of the Lord is, there is Liberty."

"That's what we want," I thought.

I, as well as a lot of other people, had been bound to plans, programs and grand schemes to operate the church for many years. It was going to be a refreshing experience to let the Holy Ghost do all that now. I looked forward to what He was going to do.

NINE
God's Healing Power at Work

The word "charismatic" wasn't in vogue in 1964. As far as most denominational people were concerned, anybody who professed to believe in the full gospel was a "holy roller." That put me and the fledgling congregation of Liberty Baptist Church into the same pot with a wild assortment of spiritual weirdness.

Bizarre stories circulated among denominational folks about us. One of the tales went something like this: "Have you heard about those holy rollers? Brother Sumrall is in charge of them. He's a pitiful preacher. He used to have a good ministry but just kinda lost his mind and went off with the holy rollers. He's out there in a little store building next door to a liquor store. Lord only knows what'll happen to him next."

I guess the situation did look a little strange. I had been pastoring a prestigious church—third largest out of sixty-four Baptist churches in the Pensacola area. Now people were saying I was crazy, a nut. Some people honestly thought I had lost my mental faculties.

Baptist preachers called me up saying they were having prayer meetings for me. "Praise the Lord," I replied happily. "I

91

need all the prayer I can get."

Once a Baptist preacher telephoned asking seriously, "Ken, have you tested the spirits?"

"I believe so, brother," I answered.

"Well, you know I John 4:1-2 says believe not every spirit but try the spirits whether they are of God . . . ," he suggested.

I laughed. "Brother, I believe Jesus Christ came in the flesh," I said freely.

"Oh, I don't mean that," he remarked. "I mean when you get off in that *frenzy*."

"I understand your concern but, really, I don't go into a frenzy. You know as well as I do that most preachers need something in these days—even a frenzy is better than deadness."

He didn't respond.

"Jesus is more real to me than He's ever been," I continued, "but I certainly don't want to put you down. I appreciate your prayers. Keep in touch."

Baptists seemingly couldn't tolerate us because we had stuck the name *Baptist* on our church. Few pentecostals accepted us because they presumed the Baptist name tag meant we believed in eternal security. Liberty Baptist Church was maligned from both directions. Fortunately for us, the blessing of the Lord was evident from the beginning.

I have always looked for new and different ideas to reach people. Now seemed like a ripe time for a small storefront church to have a radio program. It appealed to me as a good way to answer some of the confusion over us.

Selecting a popular radio station, I purchased fifteen minutes of air time following the Paul Harvey news broadcast. I never prepared any canned messages for the program called "Liberty Talks." I just sat down in front of a microphone and spoke from my heart. It was excellent timing. Response was evident from the first program.

"I'm a Baptist preacher whose been baptized in the Holy Ghost," I told my audience, "and I just want to talk to you about what God is doing today. If you've got any questions, you can call the station or our church and I'll answer them over the air."

That kind of free-wheeling invitation produced letters and phone calls aplenty. "Why did you locate next to a liquor store?" was one of the first and most frequent questions.

"I guess you can get the old wine in one place and the new wine in another," I suggested. "Folks can take their choice."

Another persistent question involved money. "Where are you getting your money? We heard you're getting it from Houston."

"It's coming from a lot further than Houston," I assured my listeners. "It's coming all the way from heaven."

Lives were touched innumerable ways through the radio program. Many received the Baptism in the Holy Spirit when they came to the storefront. Others were affected different ways.

One day I was on the air when I looked across the studio and into the glass-enclosed area where the disc jockey sat. The announcer, a young man with curly blonde hair and direct blue eyes, sat crying. I finished the program and opened the control room door before leaving. Tears brimmed in his eyes.

"Is there anything wrong?" I asked.

He removed his headphones, flipped an auto switch and looked at me. "Most of the time when preachers come in here, all they ever do is scream into the microphone," he said tearfully. "But there's something about your program. I've been listening to you every day you've been here . . . and I need to get saved. I've just gotten a powerful desire to be saved."

"Well, let me tell you about Jesus," I offered, stepping into the control room. "He's the answer to what you need."

"I'm ready to listen," he said, extending his hand.

Within a matter of minutes, the young announcer had received the Lord into his life. That was typical of the radio program's results.

Bill Gulledge, a backslidden Methodist preacher, and his wife, Joyce, heard me over the radio and were drawn to the storefront church. During the service that night, I walked out to the audience, laid hands on Joyce and prayed in the Spirit.

As I did, she screamed a blood-curdling cry.

The atmostphere was so free in the midst of her screaming everybody else praised God. I didn't understand what had happened until the next day when she telephoned explaining she had passed a kidney stone doctors had recently said would have to be removed surgically. The healing convinced her husband of God's mighty power. He repented and came back to the Lord.

During the remainder of 1964, I had several revivals scheduled in Baptist churches. One was at Green's Creek Baptist Church, outside Hattiesburg, where I had preached years before. I was unsure about cancelling the meeting but I decided to go ahead and not say anything about my new experience with the Holy Spirit.

Occasionally when the pastor and I visited homes that week, I anointed several people with oil and prayed over them. Nobody seemed to object. Yet returning home, I began to feel as if I had deceived the people. I had appeared to be something I wasn't.

"Lord, I"ll just tell the rest of the churches about my experience," I said, committing the matter to God, "and if they want to cancel, that's fine. I'll just consider that the direction You want me to take."

A revival with Ralph Branham at Kushler, Alabama, outside Mobile, was next on my calendar. I planned to call Ralph, an old friend, about the situation, but before I could, he telephoned one day. "Ken, our meeting is coming up in a few days," he announced.

"Yeah, Ralph, I've been planning on calling you," I said. "Something's happened to me since I last saw you that might change things. I've been baptised in the Holy Ghost and I speak in tongues."

The phone lines jangled with static. Ralph didn't say a word.

"Now, Ralph, I want to give you a chance to cancel this meeting because I don't want to hurt you or your ministry. So don't feel bad. I don't want to do any damage over there. Please, just feel free to tell me and we'll cancel the meeting."

"Ken, I think I ought to come over and talk with you," he suggested after a long pause.

The next day, Ralph, a lean, well-dressed fellow, drove to Pensacola. We went to the prayer room overlooking the storefront for prayer. After we had prayed for some while, Ralph spoke. His eyes were filled with tears. "Ken, I believe God wants you to come," he said.

"Are there any strings attached?" I asked.

"No."

"Ralph, I'll try my best to be a gentleman but if God moves on me to talk about the baptism, I want to be able to do so. If I want to talk about healing, is that okay?"

"Yeah. We'll just trust God."

The meetings at Ralph's church, a medium-sized Baptist congregation, that met in a drafty, white-boarded Victorian building, got off to an unusual start. At first, I preached on salvation the first three nights but the Lord — strangely enough — wouldn't allow me to open my Bible. I quoted Scriptures freely though. People responded warmly. Attendance was good.

By mid-week, I felt I should preach on confessing your faults one to another (James 5:16). It was similar to what Dr. Gene

Williams had done years before at Boulevard Baptist. I hoped to get the same results.

"A confession meeting can be a dangerous thing when people confess things that hurt others," I explained to a slightly-nervous congregation. "I don't want anybody doing that. But I'm going to sit down and if you think you've done anything that would keep God from bringing revival here you should stand up and confess it."

I guess maybe I hit the congregation a little heavy or too quickly. The church got quiet. Nobody hardly moved. Two minutes passed. Then, four. Then, five.

Finally, a plump woman in an all-green outfit and an unusually large hat, stood up in the choir loft. "I've been mad at God because He didn't answer my prayer about my mother. I prayed that my mother would live and she died. I've been holding that against the Lord. I'm sure it has affected my attitude in this church. I want to confess that and I want the people of this church to forgive me."

Her confession broke the ice. For the next two hours, people stood confessing their misdeeds, apologizing and weeping. The dam had broken loose. Revival was underway.

That same night, a young woman, thin and raven-haired, stood up and began confessing a problem in a low, muffled voice. Ralph nudged me as she spoke. "That woman is Barbara Berry. She has a four-month-old son with a heart condition. It's due for an operation and there's a fifty-fifty chance it will not live even if the operation is performed."

The service closed that night but I couldn't get Barbara or her baby out of my thoughts. The next morning, I woke still thinking about them. Ralph was already sitting at the kitchen table sipping a steaming cup of coffee when I walked in.

"Ralph, where does that woman live who has the baby with the heart condition?" I asked, taking a seat opposite him.

"About five miles out in the country," he answered, pouring me a cup.

"What would you think about us going out there and praying for that baby?" I questioned.

"Fine with me."

An hour later we left, stopping off to pick up another preacher, Harvey Golden, an energetic, rail-thin man. When we arrived at Barbara's house, a simple, wooden farm house, surrounded by tall oaks and pines, I said, "Men, I don't think the Lord wants us to be noisy about this. I think He just wants us to meditate in silence over this baby."

They all nodded in agreement.

The tiny baby, wrapped in a sky blue blanket, was asleep in a white bassinet when Ralph, Harvey and I walked into the comfortable living room. "Barbara, we came mainly to pray for the baby but we want to meditate in quiet and pray silently. Is that all right with you?"

"Yes sir," she answered, brushing her dark hair away from her pretty face.

After a few minutes of silent prayer, the words of Mark 16:17, 18 came to my mind. I opened my Bible and read softly:

"And these signs shall follow them that believe; In My name shall they cast out devils; they shall speak with new tongues; they shall take up serpents; and if they drink any deadly thing, it shall not hurt them; they shall lay hands on the sick, and they shall recover."

Barbara watched me closely, hanging on the words I read. "The Bible says *they* shall lay hands on the sick and *they* shall recover," I emphasized. "Barbara, do you believe that verse."

She looked at me seriously. "I believe the whole Bible," she said firmly.

"They shall lay hands on the sick and they shall recover," I read again. "But do you believe that verse?"

"If it's in the Bible, I believe it," she responded.

"Oh, it's in the Bible all right," I said smiling. "I just read it. That verse means that you as a believer can lay hands on your little baby and he will be healed. Do you believe that?"

"Oh, I don't know about that."

"Do you want your baby healed?" I asked.

"You know I do."

"Okay," I instructed. "I want you to go over to the bassinet and lay hands on your baby if you believe this. I'm going to lay hands on you, but I don't want you to lay hands on this baby unless you believe this verse."

Barbara's hot tears dropped onto the sleeping infant as she stood over the bassinet. The tiny form stirred. She reached out her trembling hands several times as if to touch the baby but drew them back each time.

"Lord, You know how badly I want my baby healed," she said through the tears.

Finally, she gathered her courage, reached and placed her hands on the baby. As she did, it was as if a glowing light had been turned on inside of her. Her countenance changed completely. "Brother Ken, God healed him," she began to say, tears glistening in her eyes. "I know He did. God healed my baby."

Barbara started walking around the room praising God and hugging everybody. I turned to her. "That's not all that verse says," I reminded her. "It also says they shall speak with new tongues. Would you like to do that too?"

Immediately she sank to her knees and began confessing her sins.

"No, this isn't sin confessing time," I said, taking her hand and helping her up. "This is rejoicing time. You just rejoice and receive the baptism."

Barbara began praising and glorifying God. Instantly she

was speaking in another language. Jesus had baptized her in the Holy Spirit.

Ralph Branham, watching with eyes the size of half-dollars, had never heard anyone speaking in tongues before. He jumped to his feet saying, "Now I've heard it with my own ears. I want it too."

Harvey and I both had to get back to Kushler to keep appointments but Ralph couldn't contain himself. Driving along, he suddenly announced, "Stop the car, I've got to pray."

Hurriedly he got out of the car, climbed a fence and walked up and down a plowed field asking God to baptize him in the Holy Spirit. Ralph didn't actually receive then, but he did a few weeks later in Pensacola at our all-day Thursday prayer meeting.

That night when I called for personal testimonies, Barbara was the first person to stand. "God healed my baby this morning," she said excitedly. "I know He did. I've got an appointment with the doctor tomorrow. He's going to x-ray my baby's heart and I'll have the proof tomorrow night that my baby was healed."

People sat watching her in disbelief. Nobody in the church had ever given a testimony like that, it seemed. But the next night as she had promised, Barbara had the evidence.

"I went to the doctor today with my baby," she announced, x-rays in her hands. "They examined and x-rayed my little boy. There is no sign of any defect whatsoever in his heart. Praise God."

That Baptist crowd—throwing years of tradition aside—stood applauding and praising God.

After word of that healing got around, crowds jammed the church each night. The revival was scheduled to close Friday night but the people wanted more. I went back to Pensacola on Sunday but returned on Monday. Tuesday night, I asked, "How many of you believe that God has done something special here?"

Every hand in the house shot up. Amens chorused through the building.

"Okay, tomorrow night, I'll tell you why."

Once again, the church filled up. Extra chairs lined the aisles. People stood around the back. I gave my testimony explaining about the work of the Holy Spirit and the availability of the baptism. People flocked to the altar to receive.

God had done an unbelievable work during those two weeks. He was revealing His mighty healing power to His people. Few of us would ever be the same again—even in tiny, backwater spots like Kushler . . . the Spirit was moving.

Word was soon spreading fast about the Baptist preacher who prayed for the sick. Cars soon lined the block around the little storefront church on Cervantes Street during services.

One Sunday morning, a tall, broad-shouldered man stood up in the back of the building as the service opened. "Brother Sumrall, I don't want to interrupt the church service but I'm Tom Johnson. I'm an attorney from Chipley. I heard that you prayed for babies over here and I've got a little boy here with me this morning. He's four-years-old and he's got a heart problem. We just recently had him over at the University of Florida. Doctors there said he'll die before he's nine. Would you pray for him today when you finish the service?"

The man's words struck my heart. "We'll pray for him right now," I responded. "Bring him up to the front."

Dressed in a somber gray suit, the man picked up his blonde-headed son and brought him forward. "Brother, God heals babies mainly through their parents," I explained. "The Scripture verifies that Jesus prayed for babies mainly through their parents. So I want you to lay hands over the baby's heart. I'm going to lay my hands on you and God's going to heal this child."

The man nodded his head in agreement and I began praying. As I prayed, the child jumped in his father's arms. "Daddy, something happened inside of me," he exclaimed.

The next week, that child was taken back to the University of Florida Hospital for an examination. Doctors verified there was no sign of any heart defect. God had healed him instantly!

Shortly after that, a woman telephoned from Tallahassee identifying herself as one of the governor's secretaries. "Are you the Southern Baptist preacher that prays for the sick?" she asked.

"I'm one of them," I admitted.

"I've got a little boy that's deaf in one ear and he's just started to school this year," she said. "He can't hear properly and has to sit right under the teacher's desk. Do you believe the Lord can heal him?"

"Sure," I answered.

"Would you pray for him?" she questioned.

"Sure. Will you bring him to Pensacola?"

"I guess so."

Two weeks later on a Saturday afternoon, the woman, her husband and the half-deaf child arrived at the storefront. I attempted to explain about the service the next day. I didn't want them to be frightened. As they started to leave, the little boy turned to me. "Are you going to heal me?" he asked softly, his wide brown eyes shining.

I took his small hands in mine. "Would you pray this prayer with me?"

"Okay," he said.

"Lord Jesus, thank You for healing me tomorrow in the morning service." The boy repeated the prayer and the three left the building.

The next morning they were back bright and early. The husband, a long-time Southern Baptist, shied away from coming to the front. His wife, a gregarious woman with dark auburn hair and flashing green eyes, brought the child down. "Now I want you to put your fingers in this child's ears so he can't hear anything," I instructed. Then I laid my hands on the mother and prayed.

Placing my hand over my own mouth so the boy couldn't read my lips, I looked at him saying, "Son, can you hear me?"

"Yes, sir."

"Say praise the Lord," I said.

"Praise the Lord," he responded.

The church erupted with people shouting, singing and praising the Lord. The mother was right in the middle of it all. She went to the prayer room and received the Baptism in the Holy Spirit too.

The next week she telephoned. "I just want you to know my son went back to school yesterday. He didn't have to sit by the teacher's desk any longer. He told the teacher that Jesus had healed his ear and he then took a seat in the back of the room."

The day of God's miraculous works had not passed. It was still being done—even in a humble storefront church next door to a liquor store in Pensacola, Florida.

TEN
"Is Everybody Gonna Leave?"

During the first year of operations, 1964, the Sumralls got the leftovers from the offering plate. For eight or nine months, that proved adequate. Then, December came. Many people sunk their money into Christmas presents instead of the work of the Lord.

"Honey, I've got about eight hundred dollars in bills and all I've got is thirty-five dollars from the offering for the whole month," Wanda announced one day, a worried look on her face.

"Thirty-five dollars won't even make the house payment," I mumbled.

"Well, what am I going to do?" she asked seriously.

"Just sit down and write a check to Jesus for thirty-five dollars," I suggested, after looking over the checkbook. "If we starve, we'll just blame it on the Lord."

"How're we going to do that?" she questioned.

"Well, the Lord likes missions," I responded, "just give the thirty-five dollars to missions."

"Okay," she reluctantly agreed, but nonetheless wrote out a

103

check to a missionary project of the church.

It was our last penny but we had agreed to trust God in the beginning and trust God we would do. In a few days, our faith was rewarded—the Lord answered. Eight hundred dollars in checks came through the mail. It was another lesson in God's faithfulness. The money hadn't come through the offering plate as it had normally. It came a different route, but it was still from God. Sowing and reaping was a Bible principle that worked.

More than anything else the folks meeting at Liberty Baptist Church wanted to be free. It seemed as if we had been wrapped in a cocoon of denominational rigidity all our lives. Most people welcomed the new-found freedom. Some, mired in years of tradition, had a tougher time adjusting to the new forms.

Elaine Brown, who had been my secretary at Boulevard Baptist, was the picture of propriety—trim and thin, straight-laced and mannerly. Although she had left Boulevard when I did, she reluctantly responded to our "freer" services, especially the more emotional ones.

Services had only been underway a couple of months when the Lord impressed me to begin praying for the sick one Sunday night. A line of people surrounded the platform. When I reached my wife, the Lord said, "She's going to fall over."

I stepped behind her and sure enough, she toppled over gracefully. A gasp went up from the audience, as I caught her in my arms.

Afterwards, Elaine walked to the front. Wanda was still "out" on the floor. She looked at my wife, then back at me. "Have we come to this?" she asked wearily.

"Sure looks like it," I agreed, a broad grin on my face.

A week later in a similar healing line, Elaine toppled over. Her dignity and a physical illness were healed at the same time.

She never asked, "Have we come to this?" again. She *knew* we had.

As much as anybody, I got caught up in this new-found freedom. I felt anything organized wasn't free. Consequently we had as little organization as possible. No membership. "Let the Holy Ghost lead" was our constant exhortation.

Yet in the process of being free, matters began to get out of hand. One Sunday morning, nine messages in tongues came forth. Instead of contributing to the flow of the meeting, the prophetic words were irrelevant, and most times extraneous.

"This is really getting out of hand," I thought to myself, driving home that day. "I need to do some teaching or something to clear up this problem."

I had already studied various books, as well as the Bible on the gifts of the Holy Spirit. I determined to teach on the use *and* the limitations of the gifts. One Wednesday night, I began with about forty people in the audience.

"Now the Spirit of the prophet is controlled by the prophet," I declared midway through the teaching after I had briefly laid the scriptural groundwork for the study.

Looking to my left, I saw one of the front benches swaying, almost ready to overturn. A short, heavy-set woman with dark black hair had her hands on the back of the bench. Her knuckles were white. Her eyes closed. I quickly stopped.

"Brother Ken, if I don't give it out when I get it, I get frustrated," she lamented.

"Well, I sympathize with you, sister," I answered softly, "because I get frustrated *when* you give it out."

A few people laughed. The bench stopped swaying. Some of the more spiritual women didn't think my remark was funny though. The meeting broke up in a state of tension.

Problems continued. Frequently visitors walked into the building and before they could take a seat, somebody was prophesying over them. Everytime I witnessed that, I ached inside. I knew the church was headed for trouble.

Whenever I tried to bring a word of correction, a couple of women had a pat answer for me. "Oh, Brother Sumrall, it took you a long time to understand the baptism," they'd say condescendingly. "You'll understand all this stuff after awhile."

I knew I was green as grass in this new spiritual realm but something continually suggested these activities were excessive. I felt a deep responsibility to pastor and teach the congregation. Yet, at times, I struggled with the nagging thought I might not be where God wanted me.

"Maybe I ought to get into full-time evangelistic work," I pondered many times. Several opportunities had presented themselves but I had declined each one after weighing them seriously. "Maybe I need to reconsider one of those offers," I told myself.

Ralph Branham and another Baptist pastor, Charles Simpson, met with me regularly for a time of prayer and mutual sharing. Actually I had met Charles at seminary in New Orleans and we had subsequently preached revivals in each other's church— Charles at Boulevard in Pensacola and me at Bayview Heights in Mobile.

During that revival at Ralph's church in Kushler, Charles had appeared one night and I gave him a copy of my testimony tape. He told me later he went home, stuffed towels under the door and listened to the tape. In time, Charles became a cherished friend, received the baptism at one of the all-day Liberty prayer meetings on Thursday, and began hauling carloads of people from Mobile to Pensacola to receive thereafter.

I trusted Charles and Ralph as I did few preachers. Being pastors of Baptist congregations, they understood the problems and pressures of *that* job. One Saturday night, I poured my heart out to them over the situation.

"Oh, Lord, help Ken know the mind of God," they prayed over me. "Help him to know Your direction."

We had been together most of the day praying, reading the Bible, sharing and meditating. It was past two o'clock in the morning when I felt God speaking to me. "If you don't want crying babies, you won't have a growing family," the Spirit said.

What relief those words brought me. "Thank You, Jesus," I rejoiced. "Thank You, Lord."

At first, I thought maybe I wasn't mature enough to handle this situation—maybe I was even thinking of running from the responsibility of the situation. But now, I knew I was on the right road. Even though Liberty and myself were experiencing growing pains, I was determined to continue on.

"Now—you go back and teach My people lovingly and faithfully My Word," the Lord exhorted, "and I will purge those who will not be taught."

Faithfully I returned to Pensacola and continued the series on use and limitations of the gifts of the Spirit. I knew I was walking a tightwire act without a net underneath me. I desperately wanted to keep the meetings free. Yet in trying to stamp out "wildfire," I didn't want to douse *all* the fire.

But sure enough as I preached, people began to leave. Some went back to pentecostal churches. A few left town. Others just dropped out completely. Their ears, it seemed, were dull of hearing.

A hundred and one persons had come that record-breaking Sunday. Now—vacant chairs stared back at me during each service. In a few months' time, half of the congregation had vanished.

Irene Cederstrom, one of Liberty's most avid supporters, had been a prominent member of a respectable Methodist church. A slow-talking, yet active woman, she held an important position with the Navy. One Sunday after church, she walked up. "Brother Ken, is everybody gonna leave?" she questioned, referring to the sparse attendance that morning.

"No, I don't think so, sister," I answered smiling.

"That's good," she responded, seemingly relieved.

I patted her on the back. "I was talking to God this morning anyway," I continued, "and He said He was going to stay. I'm going to stay. How about you?"

"Oh, I'm going to stay too," she assured me. "I was just wondering."

Incredibly, the drop in attendance came as the church had launched out in faith signing a contract for the purchase of a small tract of land on 57th Avenue. The manager of the ABC liquor store continually moaned about Liberty Baptist Church being located next door to his place. A portly, barrel-chested man, who constantly chewed on an unlit cigar, he frequently suggested, "You're ruining my business."

"No—I'm not trying to do that," I always answered.

"Yeah, but people see a church next door and they're ashamed to come in here and buy whiskey. Why don't you just buy the whole building or either move some place else?"

"I'd rather stay here and just make people feel bad for buying your whiskey," I grinned.

"Jeepers, creepers," he groaned, biting off the end of his cigar.

Either the Lord decided to give us a better location, or else He became sympathetic to the liquor store manager's plight—I'm not sure which. At any rate, a year after we began services in the store building, our lease ran out.

The property on 57th Avenue had a small frame house, but it wasn't suitable for a church building. I planned to sell $25,000 in bonds to construct our own building. But now with half our congregation gone, even our most ardent supporters were highly skeptical.

"Who're you going to sell those bonds to?" people continually asked. "Nobody in Pensacola trusts us. Most folks consider us with that crowd that sells prayer cloths and miracle billfolders. They aren't going to buy any bonds from us."

The people who weren't negative about the bonds simply had no money to buy them. "Well, if God's in it, it'll work out," I found myself answering many times. I was being pushed to the test, but I was determined to do my part. Thereafter, I knocked on doors and talked to people.

It was up to God now whether Liberty Baptist Church had its own building.

The first Liberty Church building on Cervantes Street located next door to the liquor store, 1964.

The first members of Liberty Church.

ELEVEN

False Prophetesses, Hobo Prophets and Holy Ghost Tooth Fillers

God *was* leading the sale of the church bonds, and miraculously, every bond sold. Work was thrown into high gear on our new building. Our lease ran out on Cervantes Street and we had to move into the new facilities even before it was completed. A year had passed since services began in the store building, Liberty Baptist Church now had its own building—a spare 34 by 125 foot concrete-block structure.

People truly had to love God to join us in the new building. All we had finished were the walls and a roof. There was no electricity, bathroom facilities or much of anything else. An Army barracks looked like a plush room at the Ritz compared to what we had.

But in a few weeks, crews of men from the church worked nights to get the building finished. Like everybody else, I pitched in digging ditches for gas pipes and putting beams into place. Few people in the congregation were without blisters or sore muscles from all the labor.

The new building was designed to hold two hundred people. "You'll never grow to fill up this place," the skeptics suggested.

Even though we'd lost a number of people, I doubted the skeptics. I felt God had an imposing challenge for us. I was beginning to recognize possibilities in ministry that I had never seen before.

Yet as we explored new avenues of ministry, problems from the past continually stepped in our way. Some of the extremes that began in the storefront had followed us to the new location. The problems were more serious than people just speaking in tongues out of turn in a service. Three women felt as if they had a personal word from God for everybody. One in particular led the others. She didn't just give out "God bless you" prophecies. It was *directive* prophecy.

"God wants you to go over to Mrs. Jones' house today and drive her to Mobile," she prophesied at times, or "God doesn't want you to attend this revival meeting. He wants you someplace else."

One Sunday night, a tanned and youthful-looking man walked into the service while I was preaching. Something sinister about him instantly bound my efforts. I couldn't understand what happened but my thoughts wouldn't come. I lost all ability to keep the audience's attention. I stopped and called the people to prayer.

As I did, the church's troublesome prophetess, Ruth Flatstone, walked to the man and began prophesying over him. When she finished, he was a combination of Oral Roberts and Billy Graham. "A chosen vessel, you will have an anointed ministry and win millions to the Lord," she prophesied with great exuberance.

I didn't believe a word she said. Afterwards, I confronted her. "I don't witness to any of that prophecy you spoke over that man," I said emphatically.

Her eyes tightened, her mouth turned downward. "Oh, God doesn't lie," she said defensively.

"I know God doesn't lie," I answered, "but that doesn't mean your prophecy was necessarily God speaking."

"Well, I don't miss God," she replied.

"Your problem isn't that you're prophesying all the time," I suggested, feeling the Lord trying to reach out to the woman. "Your problem is you're *never* wrong."

Her eyes widened and she walked off in a huff.

The following day, that same man she had prophesied over robbed a service station in Pensacola and was promptly arrested. News reports identified him as an escaped convict. When I recited all the facts for Ruth Flatstone, she responded, "Well, I don't know what God meant but I know God doesn't lie."

"No," I said firmly, "you're wrong on this and you really need to admit it to yourself."

"Well, maybe the man's going to have a ministry in prison or something," she offered. "I don't know. I just know God doesn't lie."

I shook my head. "Sister, I think you're grabbing at straws," I admonished her. "I think you're dead wrong about this."

No correction helped whatsoever. The problem persisted.

Hidden from me was the fact she was prophesying over many women in the church. On Friday, she called a select few to give them the *special* word for the day. One particular Friday, Joyce Barry, a young woman in the group, decided she was going to spend the morning in prayer. She took the phone off the hook for privacy.

About noon, a neighbor knocked on Joyce's door. "Mrs. Flatstone is trying to get in touch with you. She said to tell you to put your phone back on the hook. She wants to talk with you."

Joyce hesitantly did so and in a few seconds the phone rang. "What's up?" Mrs. Flatstone asked in a strained voice.

"I just took the phone off the hook to pray this morning,"

Joyce answered.

"Well, you missed God because I had a word for you," Mrs. Flatstone said loftily. "God had something to say to you but you just missed it. Don't ever do that again."

"Uh, if you'll excuse me," Joyce replied, "I just don't receive that as being from the Lord. I think God wanted me to pray this morning."

"No, no—God didn't want you to do that," Mrs. Flatstone interrupted.

"I reject that," Joyce said firmly, hanging up the phone.

In about an hour, Mrs. Flatstone appeared at Joyce's door with another woman from the ladies' group. Sarah Miller, the other woman, laid hands on Joyce and prophesied. Mrs. Flatstone, a short, plump woman with reddish-brown hair, interpreted.

"God is grieved at you my daughter for rejecting my prophetess," she said in an emotion-filled voice.

Joyce stood up hastily. "Wait a minute," she shouted. "Stop this nonsense. I don't receive any of this and I don't want you women here. I tried to be polite by allowing you to come in but I don't receive this."

The two women left in a burst of angry words at Joyce.

Sunday night, Joyce was at the church altar praying when Mrs. Flatstone walked up behind her. "The Lord says there is no need to pray until you apologize to the prophetess," she said knowingly, "because He will not hear you anymore—ever—until you apologize."

Joyce was in tears when she explained the story to me. A holy rage rose up inside me. I honestly believe it was the Holy Spirit getting furious. I went into the sanctuary and brought Mrs. Flatstone to my small office.

"I've got a prophecy for you," I said strongly. "God is going to take you out of this city and take you away from these women you're controlling. He is going to take you from this city because if you went to another church you'd still try to control them. I'm not going to allow this situation anymore. I am breaking your power right now."

She looked at me for a moment, then left the room without a word. Within a week, her husband was abruptly transferred to Louisiana and they moved. My prophecy *did* come true.

Even then, she wrote letters to women in the church trying to control their activities. One day I wrote her a long letter outlining all the false prophecies she had given. She had called harlots to preach. She had prophesied over people not to attend meetings at Liberty. She had worked against the church from many levels. If any church speaker said something she didn't like, she quickly spread the word not to attend his meetings.

I also included a second letter to her. It said simply, "If you ever write back here trying to control these women with prophecies or any other kind of word, I am going to post the first letter on the bulletin board and let our people know all the silly stuff you've done."

That broke her power completely. She never sent another letter.

But just as the church and I had problems with false prophetesses within the congregation, I also faced difficulties with migrating "hobo" prophets. Since we had become free in the spirit, we wanted to be open to anybody—in spite of appearances—who might have a word from God.

Many of the wanderers we allowed in the pulpit were no more prophets of God than the man in the moon. They were simply free-spirited, roaming vagabonds with the gift of gab who spoke in biblical lingo for our benefit. Traveling with threadbare clothes, a worn Bible and a battered suitcase, they floated into town, gave a special word at Liberty and then expected us to care for them for the duration of their stay. The biggest problem was they wouldn't work.

Hiriam Chosen, a short, strong-willed man in his early fifties, was one hobo prophet in particular. Dirty, unshaven and reeking of an unbelievable odor, he always seemed ready to deliver a "word from God" whenever he traveled through Pensacola.

Any service where Chosen was in attendance was always punctuated by a long, rambling prophecy from him. Afterwards, he sat in the audience reading his Bible completely ignoring the preacher, who in most cases was me.

Several times he had wandered through Pensacola mooching off people in the congregation and "showing off" in the church. Finally, I faced up to the fact I had to deal with him—prophet or not.

One night after several people had complained about him, I took Hiriam aside for a chat. "We're going to have to make some changes," I began, attempting to be diplomatic.

"Changes? What're you talking about?" he responded, heating up almost immediately.

"Well, every time you show up around here we have problems," I suggested, "and that's got to change."

"Problems? I don't understand what you're talking about."

Now—I was beginning to heat up. "In that case, let me spell it out for you then." His bushy eyebrows rose a notch as I spoke.

"When you come here, I want you to get a bath and be clean," I instructed firmly. "If you can't do that on your limited finances, then get a job and buy some decent clothes. You can do that. You're an able-bodied man."

His dark, lined face turned to a scowl. "Why you're rejecting a genuine man of God," he reacted bitterly.

"No—nobody's rejecting anything," I responded. "I'm just

calling your attention to what the Bible says. If a man won't work, he shouldn't eat. That applies to traveling prophets too."

Chosen took my attempt at correction as total rejection. Instead of listening, he hit the road. That was the last I ever saw of him.

After being bitten by the likes of Hiriam Chosen and several of his counterparts, one would think I'd learn not to court the hobo prophets. Yet one cold, rain-soaked day, I was driving down Fairfield Drive when I saw a thin, tubercular-looking man limping along the roadside. He appeared to have a crippled leg. I stopped, backed up my car and rolled down the window. "You need a ride?" I asked.

"Yeah—sure do."

"Where you headed?" I questioned as the man got in beside me.

"Oh, I'm headed for the bus stop," he explained. "I had to come across town to get my welfare check. I've moved and the address ain't been changed yet...you know how that goes, I guess."

"Well, just give me the directions and I'll get you home," I volunteered.

The shabbily-dressed man identified himself as Elijah Hardy. When I introduced myself, he smiled warmly. "Oh yeah, you're the Baptist preacher whose got the Holy Ghost. I've been wanting to come hear you preach."

"Where do you go to church, Elijah?" I asked, maneuvering the car through traffic.

He shrugged his shoulders. "I just go here and there," he said nonchalantly. "I don't have any transportation. That's my main problem. I'd go more often otherwise."

"That's no problem," I offered. "I'll get somebody to pick you up if you'd like to come to Liberty."

He smiled. "Yeah, that sounds nice," he agreed. "I'd appreciate that."

It was a suggestion I would live to regret. Elijah became an irritating nuisance in record-breaking time. In the men's Bible class, he was constantly interrupting the teacher. While I was in the pulpit delivering a sermon, he loudly finished my sentences for me. I struggled to be polite with him—holding back my tongue a number of times. He clearly had the Midas touch in reverse. Everything he touched died!

One Sunday night right in the middle of a deeply-moving altar call, people were streaming forward. The Holy Spirit was moving in a powerful way. Elijah leaped out of his chair screaming at the top of his lungs.

"I've got the anointing of God on me," he shouted, hands waving in the air. "Come on down here folks and I'll get you healed."

Quickly—the Holy Spirit vanished out the door and the bewildered people returned to their seats. Elijah had mortally wounded the service.

"Did you know what you did tonight?" I asked, confronting him after the meeting.

"No," he said, seemingly puzzled by my question.

"You killed the service."

"I killed the service?"

"Yes sir, you sure did."

"How'd I do that?"

"By speaking out of turn."

"Well, can't a man speak when the Holy Ghost wants him to around here?"

"Sure, but do you know anything about flow?"

"*Flow*? What do you mean flow?"

"I mean we flow together as a body of people," I tried to explain. "When the Holy Ghost speaks, the body feels it. It's not a matter of every individual trying to get the mind of God. We try to get the mind of God together. We flow together."

He nodded his head. "That's no problem, I can do that."

"But flowing together means we don't interrupt one another," I continued. "That's what you're doing. Evidently you were trained that way and maybe that's okay in some places. I don't want to hurt your feelings but I don't want you doing that anymore."

"Yes sir."

"When I call for testimonies in the future, I don't want a twenty minute sermon from you. When the men's class in underway, I don't want you constantly interrupting. The same goes for the church service."

Elijah was clearly upset when he walked off but he continued attending the services. Then, the correction I applied began to wear off. A few weeks later, another free-flowing move of the Spirit came. Most of the congregation was gathered at the altar praying. Elijah was soon out of his seat and praying too—rattling the rafters like a cannon as he did. People looked around unsure of what was happening. Gradually, the altar call died.

I went home that night perplexed over the situation. Before falling asleep, I laid Elijah at the feet of Jesus. "Lord, You've got to do something about this situation...even if You have to take him home like You did the original Elijah in a chariot of fire!"

The next morning I remembered a Free Holiness church that had recently closed its doors. "I wonder if my trouble-making friend and that church have any connection?" I asked myself.

I decided to check it out and drove to Elijah's house. He welcomed me warmly. "You really want to preach, don't you," I asked, taking a seat.

He smiled broadly showing gaps where teeth once were. "Oh, praise God, I do," enthused, clapping his hands together.

At first, Elijah must have thought I was going to ask him to assist in pastoring Liberty. But his facial expression changed rapidly when I announced, "I think I've found you a place to preach. There's a Free Holiness church closed down because they don't have a preacher. These places are usually owned by one man but I think I can get you in as the preacher."

"What's the matter, brother?" he asked, surprised at my suggestion. "What's the matter?"

"Let's face it, you're a good man," I said candidly. "You love God and I'm a good man and I love God. But our ministries don't flow together. Which one of us is right is beside the point. I want to put you where you can do whatever God tells you to do and it won't bother anybody else."

"Okay," he agreed reluctantly, "if that's the way you feel about it."

Pulling on a frayed sweater, Elijah joined me in the car and we drove to the church. Franklin Smyth, a portly, dour-faced man, who owned the building and a couple of other businesses on the block, readily accepted him as the congregation's new pastor. Elijah was off and running in his first pastorate.

I don't know what happened to him after that. He never called or visited Liberty again. Some weeks later, I drove by the Free Holiness church and noticed it had been closed again. I figured Elijah must have gotten "free in the spirit" once too often.

Liberty was also frequently approached by traveling preachers and Bible teachers who wanted to hold a revival or just lead a "meetin'." "God's led me here, I know He has," more than one itinerate revivalist told me. Discerning the mind of God in those situations was never easy, especially if you were trying to be open to the Lord. I found that out when a preacher who called himself a tooth filler arrived.

"Oh, you're a dentist by profession," I suggested.

"No, I'm not a dentist," he replied. "I'm a Holy Ghost tooth filler."

Chuckling at the thought, I said, "I've never heard of one."

"Why is that so funny?" he asked.

"Well, I thought if God was going to do something He'd just give you a new tooth, not fill an old one," I answered.

"Well, I've got proof," he shot back, pulling out newspaper clippings showing he had ministered in churches throughout California.

"Is there anybody you had a meeting with in this area recently?" I questioned, wanting to check the man more thoroughly.

"Yeah. Herman Watson in New Orleans."

I called Watson on the telephone. "Do you know Marvin Fuller?" I asked.

"Yes."

"Has he been in meetings with you?"

"He just left," Watson answered.

"He says he has a ministry in filling teeth and I've never heard of anything like that before," I admitted.

"Brother, if I didn't believe in miracles, I wouldn't have a man who does," he retorted.

"Wait a minute," I said. "I *do* believe in miracles but this sounds so different I thought I'd better check it out."

"Well, it's real."

"Do you have anybody there God filled teeth for?"

"Yeah, about two hundred of them."

"Anybody close to you?"

"Yeah, my secretary."

The New Orleans preacher had given me all the right answers but I was still troubled inside. I felt a gnawing uneasiness. God was obviously trying to tell me something but all I could see was the sensational.

"If we could have a tooth filler and if he fills teeth, we're going to draw people," I reasoned, "and right now, that's what we need." The church was experiencing a bad slump and we needed a shot in the arm of some kind.

On that basis, I agreed for the Holy Ghost tooth filler to go to work. The meetings were sensational from the start. Newspaper ads proclaimed the tooth filler's arrival. The building overflowed with people.

And fillings began mysteriously appearing in people's mouths—including my own—all in gold. I had some old Army fillings that had turned black. But one day I looked and they had all turned gold. I walked around like everybody else did—my mouth wide-open showing off my new fillings.

Fuller, a tall, lean man with gray-blue eyes that always seemed to have a faraway look, never actually prayed for people. He simply touched them with his hand. My wife working as his assistant followed along behind quickly producing a clean dental mirror. Every time, the fillings had turned to gold.

His preaching was good—mostly solid evangelist messages. But to my way of thinking, he didn't say or do anything that was out of order. I just had that lingering feeling of trouble ahead. However, the meetings were so sensational and the crowds enthusiastic the tooth filler stayed an extra week.

Then, disaster struck.

A woman came to my office with a terrifying report. "I don't know what to do with this," she said unhappily, "except to tell you. I know Fuller's family. He has a wife and four children in Waco, Texas. And that woman with him is not his wife."

My heart landed on my shoetops when I heard the news. "Thanks sister," I responded. "I'll check into it...only please don't say anything about it."

"You have my word," she promised, leaving my office.

Nervously I picked up the telephone and began checking out her report. To my increasing dismay, the information proved absolutely correct. In fact, to make matters worse, the woman Fuller had introduced as his wife hadn't been attending many of our services. She had been holding meetings with local spiritualists.

I confided the situation to Wanda the next morning during our prayer time. "Wow," she moaned. "If anything like that ever hits the newspapers, we'll be buried."

"Yeah, I know," I agreed, pondering the situation. "A lot of people would probably be delighted in just that too."

"What should we do?" Wanda asked, a look of concern mirrored in her face.

"Well, I think I ought to just ease him out quietly," I decided. "There's no way I can let him stay any longer."

We prayed several additional days over the problem and then I closed the meeting. Fuller left town without any complications.

I simply wanted to forget about the whole episode until a preacher from Baton Rouge telephone several weeks later. "What do you think about this evangelist Fuller?" he asked.

"I wouldn't have him," I said bluntly. "I don't want to talk about the situation but I wouldn't have him."

"You sure that's all you've got to say?" he quizzed.

"Yeah."

"Okay," he said without pursuing it further.

The next day, the preacher called back on a three-way telephone hook-up. Fuller and the church's deacon chairman were on the other phones. "What'd you mean telling people I'm not fit to have?" the tooth filler questioned hotly.

"Brother, now you're asking for this and I'm just going to tell you like it is right over the phone," I said strongly.

"Yeah—go ahead," he dared.

"In the first place, you've got a wife and four children in Waco, Texas that you're not supporting. That's enough to say a man's not worth having in a pulpit."

"What???" he tried to interrupt.

"Secondly, you came to our church with another woman you introduced as your wife who isn't your wife," I continued. "So you're living with a woman you're not married to. Thirdly, the woman who was with you was a spiritualist and was holding meetings while you were preaching for us. And in the fourth place, all those teeth you filled have not lasted. They have all turned back the way they were. Is that enough?"

"We'll come against you with everything we've got," he screamed, raving like a madman. "I'll put a curse on you."

"I reject your curse in the Name of Jesus Christ and I say it'll boomerang on your head. And to show you I'm not afraid of you, I'm going to run your name in our church magazine and tell people we don't endorse you. You're a false prophet and a deceiver."

With that, the tooth filler slammed the phone down. "Thanks, Ken," the other pastor said. "Believe me, I'll take care of things from this end . . ."

TWELVE

Miracles on 57th Avenue

Even though there were dark, trouble-filled times of testing with the false prophetesses, hobo prophets and "supposed" Holy Ghost tooth fillers, the blessing of God continued to shine through the work of Liberty Baptist Church and its people.

At times, I felt the presence of the Holy Spirit permeate every corner of that concrete block building. There seemed to be a holy presence hovering over the place creating a unique atmosphere.

Once Dr. John Keller, a long-time friend, was attending an all-day service at the church. After he had been introduced to speak, he quickly pulled his shoes off. "I feel like I'm standing on holy ground the Holy Ghost is so thick in here," he said through an emotion-charged voice.

That same morning Dr. Keller stopped briefly in his talk and a message in tongues came forth. The interpretation said, "If you will keep the love flowing as it's flowing now, you will not have to ask Me to manifest Myself. You couldn't keep Me from manifesting Myself because I manifest Myself in an atmosphere of love."

Sometimes people were turned off by the hand-clapping, arm-waving and lusty singing at Liberty but they were continually attracted by the warmth and love. More than anything else, that seemed to characterize the Holy Spirit's ministry at Liberty.

Ethel and Ralph Lee were two people miraculously touched by the Lord through Liberty. The Lees managed the largest trailer village in the Pensacola area. It sat along the scenic highway overlooking the Gulf. Ethel had been afflicted with cancer for many years and had suffered through numerous operations and cobalt treatments. Her body was left permanently scarred. She was in constant pain.

At last, doctors told her she had "maybe" two months to live. Through friends, Ethel heard about the folks at Liberty who believed in divine healing.

"Oh, well," Ethel thought to herself. "I don't have anything else to lose. I might as well try those people out."

As always, it was easy to spot visitors in the service. That's probably true at most full gospel meetings when newcomers arrive. I went back and introduced myself to the Lees the Sunday they came. They sat through a portion of the service and then had to leave. Ethel couldn't sit for long periods of time because of the persistent pain in her body.

The next day she telephoned the church asking for me. A group of women were there at the time praying. After being told I was out of town, Ethel described her problem, "And I need prayer—soon," she said.

"That's no problem," answered Joan Brown. "We'll just close up the church and come out to pray for you."

An hour later, three of the women were seated in Ethel's living room hearing her story. "And I heard your pastor quoting a verse on Sunday," she reminded the ladies, reaching for her Bible. "I believe it's in James."

"Oh, you mean James 5:14,15," Joan suggested.

"That's right," Ethel responded finding the verses and beginning to read them outloud. "Is any sick among you? Let him call for the elders of the church; and let them pray for him, anointing him with oil in the name of the Lord: And the prayer of faith shall save the sick, and the Lord shall raise him up; and if he has committed sins, they shall be forgiven him."

Producing a bottle of oil, Ethel said, "I know you're not elders, but I've got some oil here and I'd like to be anointed ... just like the Scripture says."

Each of the three women anointed Ethel on the forehead with the oil. They began praying in unison. As they prayed, Joan abruptly asked, "Ethel, do you have a hole where one of your breasts was removed?"

"Yes," she replied.

"Is it about the size of a half-dollar?"

"Yes."

"Well, I see that hole closing up. I believe God is healing you."

And sure enough, that's what had happened. The hole where Ethel's breast was removed closed up. It was the Lord's way of demonstrating her complete healing from cancer. Doctors were astonished at her condition weeks later, and they could find no trace of cancer in her body.

Ethel's dramatic healing brought the Lees into the services at Liberty on a regular basis. It also gave many desperately sick people faith to believe God for their own miracle.

Her husband Ralph was another story. A medium-built, frail-looking man with a permanent liquored-up reddish color to his face, he had been an alcoholic for years. He had only managed to sober up for Ethel's impending death. Now that she had been healed, he didn't know what to think of her newly-inspired faith in God. The services at Liberty plainly bored him to death. He soon volunteered to cook Sunday dinner for Ethel while she went to church.

One day the Lord impressed me to visit Ralph. When I arrived, he was working with some maintenance people. In a few minutes he walked over to where I was standing. Unexplainably I found myself saying, "Ralph, if you expect to go to hell, you won't have to do a thing. You'll be in hell in two weeks."

I was shocked at my own words. Yet Ralph's poker face never changed.

"Thank-ie," he replied in his country twang, then walked off to work with the maintenance crew.

I hurried into the Lees' house and explained to Ethel what had just happened. Tears came to my eyes. I felt as if I had pronounced God's death sentence on a man.

Not quite two weeks later, I was returning from a ministry trip outside Pensacola. Tired and worn, I looked forward to a hot shower and bed. Wanda was waiting for me when I unlocked the front door.

"They've been trying to get in touch with you," she announced. "In fact I tried to reach you before you left Birmingham. Ralph Lee had a heart attack and they're not expecting him to live. They want you to come to the hospital right away."

I jumped back in the car and rushed to the hospital. Ralph was still in a trauma room in the emergency room section. Doctors had just removed him from an oxygen tent—giving him little hope of living. His already weakened heart had suffered a massive coronary, they said.

Still dressed in khaki work clothes, Ralph appeared unconscious. His face was ashen; his lips purple. Delicate monitoring equipment was strapped around his chest.

I didn't know how to pray or what to pray for. So—I simply knelt and began praying in the Spirit. Momentarily I felt a cold hand on my head. I stood up, looking into Ralph's watery eyes.

"Brother Ken, I know why I'm here," he sobbed. "If you'll pray that God will spare my life, I promise I'll come to church, get baptized and serve the Lord."

"Do you mean that with all your heart, Ralph?" I asked gently.

"Sure do."

"Okay, Ralph, I'll pray for your healing," I responded, taking his clammy hand. I prayed asking God for a miracle. Nothing short of that would prevent Ralph Lee from dying. As I prayed, peace flooded my heart.

"Ralph, I believe you're going to get out of the hospital," I predicted confidently. "I believe God has healed you. You're going to be all right."

Within a few days, Ralph was dismissed from the hospital, came to church and repented of his drinking. Everybody was in awe of God's miracle. I set a date for Ralph's baptism but before it came off he was drunk again.

This time, he was worse than ever. He stayed drunk most of the day and night. Ethel had to leave their house several times when he became violent, cursing her and blaspheming the church. In a matter of days, Ralph suffered a second heart attack and was back in the hospital's coronary unit. Once again, I went down and prayed over him.

The following Sunday night, I told the congregation Ralph was back in the hospital. "I believe we should unite in prayer and seek God on this man's behalf tonight," I exhorted the people.

As the congregation moved into prayer, I sensed a unity in the Spirit as Ralph was lifted before the Lord. Then I began praying fervently for him. As I did, the prayer moved into prophecy and I heard myself proclaiming, "Ralph Lee will be saved, healed, baptized in the Holy Ghost and become a pillar in this church."

Nobody believed the prophecy. Many people said so. In fact, I had a hard time believing it myself considering all the circumstances involved.

"It seems to me," one woman suggested, "the only way that'll happen and be permanent is for Ralph to get saved, healed, baptized and then have somebody shoot him! He'll never stand up and become a pillar in this church. I just don't believe it."

"Oh, no, you've missed God," I disagreed. "Ralph Lee's going to be saved, healed, baptised in the Holy Ghost and become a pillar in this church. There'll be no need for a gun."

"I hope you're right," she allowed, "but if I was a betting person, it's a pretty safe bet he won't last."

One day I was at home meditating and praying about Ralph when I got a strong urge to pay him a visit. He was about half-bombed when I arrived. "Ralph, I believe the Lord wants me to teach you the Bible," I announced as we sat around his breakfast table.

"Well, if that's what the Lord wants, all right," he answered, ever cordial to me.

"I'll meet you at your house across town at nine o'clock every morning and I promise to let you go exactly at ten," I said.

"All right," he agreed in a whiskey-soaked voice.

Monday morning, I started teaching Ralph the Bible. He came Tuesday and Wednesday. Each day, he sat seemingly unmoved as I taught for an hour, then left without much comment. I wasn't sure what effect this was having. "Maybe none," I pondered.

As usual, Ethel was at prayer meeting on Wednesday night. "How's Ralph doing?" I asked, looking for some hopeful signs of his changed behavior.

"Brother Ken, I hate to tell you this," she said frankly, "but I think you're wasting your time."

"Why?"

"Well, Ralph stops by the bar and gets some beer on his way back to the trailer park from your Bible lessons. He's pretty drunk by the time he gets home. You're not doing him any good. Why don't you just quit?"

Faith welled up in my heart each time I heard negative comments about Ralph's chances. "Ralph Lee's going to be saved, healed, baptised in the Holy Ghost and become a pillar in this church," I responded.

"Well.." she said, and her voice trailed off.

I could understand Ethel's doubts. She had lived with an alcoholic for many years, wrestling with him through binges and "drying out" spells. She had only just returned home in recent months to live with him because their trailer business was failing due to his drinking.

Ralph showed up for the Thursday and Friday sessions. The last day I said, "Ralph, I can't come at nine in the morning but I can be here about noon. You've been promising me a flounder dinner and tomorrow's the day if you'd like to do it."

His tanned, wrinkled face brightened into a wide grin. "I'll sure do it," he volunteered, eager to please me.

The next day Ralph prepared a sumptuous flounder dinner with all the assorted trimmings. When we finished eating, I figured I'd have the hourly Bible teaching afterwards—but the Lord had other plans.

"Do you know what I believe God wants me to do today?" I asked, pushing away my empty plate.

"What's that?" he responded.

"I believe He wants me to call two of our men, get them to meet us down at the church. I'll take you down there and we'll cast the devil out of you."

At first, Ralph eyed me suspiciously, then his face lightened. "Well, if that's what the Lord wants," he mumbled. "Okay."

The two men, both experienced in deliverence, met us later

that afternoon at the church. Ralph took a seat in what we called the "glory chair." The three of us began marching around the chair calling every demon we could think of by name. We figured Ralph had most of them.

"Devil, you can't have Ralph Lee," we chorused, walking around the chair, voices bouncing off the block walls. "He's going to be saved, healed, baptised in the Holy Ghost and become a pillar in the church."

Initially Ralph sat motionless in the chair. But after we had marched around the chair for about an hour, he began talking to the Lord. "Oh, yes, Lord, I want to be saved," he repeated tearfully. "Oh, yes, Lord, I want to be saved. I want to be free from the devil."

As Ralph joined in, I noticed his face had lightened up losing much of its hardness. Finally he looked at me saying, "Brother Ken, I believe Jesus just saved me! I never felt like this in my whole life! I never felt like this before!"

He started to stand up. "No, Brother, just keep your seat, we'll just get it all while you're here," I admonished. "I want you to be baptized in the Holy Ghost and speak in tongues."

Ralph sat back and we started marching around the chair again. "Lord, we praise You for saving Ralph Lee," we declared in unison. "Lord, we praise You for saving Ralph Lee."

Then I began instructing Ralph. "Come on, Ralph, praise the Lord for saving you. Just start praising the Lord and you'll be speaking in tongues in no time."

He started in right behind me. "Thank You Jesus for saving me," he said a little weakly at first. "Thank You Jesus for saving me." The more he praised the Lord, the stronger his voice became. Soon he was freely glorifying God. "Thank You, Jesus. Praise the Lord. Praise God."

In a few minutes, he was gloriously baptized in the Holy Spirit.

The church was electrified to say the least. Ralph Lee had been saved, healed and baptised in the Holy Spirit. The following Sunday night he was baptised in water.

Everything was going fine until two weeks later when I got a phone call. "Ralph Lee's out at the cemetery sitting on his uncle's grave crying and drinking beer," came the startled voice. "In fact, he's got a case of beer with him."

"Well, bring him in," I murmured.

An hour later, Ralph was brought to my office—beer and all. His clothes were disheveled and dirty. He reeked of beer and sweat. He could barely walk or talk. "Ralph, we're going to praise the Lord," I announced as he was poured into a chair in front of me.

"Yeah—hic—we're going—hic—to praise—the Lord," he slurred.

"We're going to praise the Lord for being so good," I said.

"Yeah—hic—we're going—hic—to do that—hic," he mumbled.

Depression had caught Ralph off guard and he began to think of an uncle who died years ago. Automatically he turned to drink. But in thirty minutes, he was back completely sober. It was his last drink. He never took another one for the rest of his life. He was totally cured.

Seven years remained to Ralph's life. In that time, the Lord's prophecy came true. Ralph Lee became a pillar at Liberty Baptist Church. Wherever he went or whatever he did, he told people about his precious Jesus.

"He's the One who saves and forgives," he always said, "even old alkys like me." Tears always drenched his rugged cheeks when he spoke about Jesus. No one could doubt it was real to Ralph Lee.

When the church's charter had been drawn up, I had included a provision for a Bible school. Liberty Bible College, I called it.

I didn't know how or when God might inaugurate such a school but in the back of my mind I always believed He would.

Early in 1966, four young men in the church—Paul Koehler, Randy Sumrall, Charles Freeman, Jimmy Weaver—came to me individually asking about Bible training. They were hungry to know the Word of God and wanted more than they'd normally get in a church program. "Could this be God?" I asked myself.

There were few full gospel Bible schools in those days. I didn't known where I might send them. The simplest solution was to hold classes four nights a week. And that's the way it all began.

I taught three courses myself—practical theology, gifts of the Holy Spirit and Old Testament survey. Beth Bishop, who had joined us a year before with her husband Bob, who himself would become a trusted assistant, taught English. In fact, the Bishops worked as a team with that class. Beth taught the students at her kitchen table while Bob baby-sat in a back bedroom.

The program was established on an 11-week basis. Since I had always attended schools on the semester system, I didn't know 11 weeks was the length of a quarter. God was leading unbeknownst to me.

That summer, I explained my ideas about a Bible school to various people in the church. All I got was blank stares and questioning looks. It seemed as if nobody could visualize the need. "It seems what you're suggesting could be done in a regular church program," many said.

Yet, when Bill Caffey, a young Baptist songleader from Texas, who had been baptized in the Holy Spirit, came to our summer convention, he was enthused about my plans.

"I can't promise you anything but hard work," I told him, "but if you'll help me at nights with the school, I believe you can get a job with the public school system during the days."

"That's fine with me," Caffey agreed.

He recognized the leading of the Lord and in a few months with his wife, Jimmie Jo, moved to Pensacola. God was beginning to fill gaps everywhere we had a need. Nobody visualized any formal academic program. It was seen as a pratical training school. I printed the first school catalog myself on an offset machine. In fact, I preached with inky hands for several weeks afterwards which proved it.

The Bible school's first full year began in September, 1966 with sixteen students enrolled. Several preachers helped out as teachers: Charles Simpson, Ralph Branham, Gene Adkins.

It was a humble beginning but I had grown accustomed to that. Each year the attendance grew though. The following year we had 36 enrolled and were climbing.

With college kids, there was always excitement too. One cold Saturday night, when I lived in a house across from the church, I was in the living room preparing myself for the next day's services.

Bam! Bam! Bam!

It was the front door. When I went to answer the knocking, it was some students. "Come quickly," they shouted, out of breath. "There's a student lying out on the campus paralyzed."

I didn't take time to dress. I simply ran across the street in my bedroom shoes as fast as I could. The student, Bob Zannini, was a young curly-headed guy from Montgomery we had helped find a simple job because he has a fused spine. Fear seemed to be controlling the five or six kids standing around him.

"What's happened?" I asked, kneeling down beside Bob.

"I guess this is it, Brother Ken," he groaned. "I can't move my arms or legs. I can't turn over."

I stood up looking around for somebody who could call an

ambulance. Even as I did, the Lord spoke to me. "I'll heal him," He said plainly, "if you'll not panic and believe Me."

"Okay, kids," I announced, turning to the students gathered around Bob, "quit praying for him to be healed now and start praising God. The Lord's going to do it."

Their pleading and begging immediately went into praise and thanks. I knelt once again beside Bob. "Are you willing for us to wait on God to heal you?" I asked. "If you're not, I'll go ahead and call an ambulance...but I believe God'll heal you."

"Yes sir," he responded, "I'll trust the Lord."

"Okay," I said calmly. "I'm going to start talking to the limbs of your body and command them to start functioning. You just thank the Lord for what He's doing."

And quickly I began with his right arm commanding it to move and operate properly. In a few minutes Bob was able to move it slowly. Then, I moved to the left arm. For some reason, that arm didn't respond immediately so I went to the right leg and got it moving. Then, I got the left leg moving. Finally, I went back to the left arm. Now it was moving.

"Let's turn him over," I instructed the students. Several burly fellows and myself shifted Bob over on his stomach. "In the Name of Jesus, you will never be fused again," I began commanding the spine. "You will never be fused again."

The anointing of God was powerful. I could fill strength flooding through Bob's body. "Let's stand him up," I told the kids.

Now, Bob was on his feet, a little wobbly at first. I started walking beside him as he trudged along a few steps, then he moved into a run. Before I knew it, he had shot past me on a dead run around the church property.

Bob Zannini had been totally healed.

The next morning I used him as a perfect sermon illustration. In fact, he ran up and down the aisle for the congregation. It was a great lesson for preachers in training about the power of God. The miracles never ceased to unfold on 57th Avenue as the Holy Spirit moved in our midst.

The second Liberty Church building on 57th Avenue, about 1970.

Ken on a missionary trip to the Philippines.

THIRTEEN
The Promised Land

Three years after we moved into the 200-seat concrete-block building on 57th Avenue, the church had outgrown it. The new facilities would have to seat at least five hundred. Once again, the men of the church worked together to do much of the construction. Fortunately, the Lord had led Elton Dreadin to our church. An experienced steel erector, he was perfect to oversee the construction.

The Jesus Movement hit during the late 1960's and that produced a spark in attendance. All across the country, kids were getting saved and coming to school at Liberty. In fact, the more I traveled around the country speaking in various meetings, it seemed the more kids came to school here.

I had always spent a lot of time away from home — traveling and ministering. When I wasn't traveling, I was swamped with work for a growing church plus a Bible college. There was always an abundance of people with problems desperately seeking my help.

One cold, windy night, just home after a week-long trip, I had stayed behind at church ministering to several people. It was about 10:30 when I finally arrived at home. Wanda was already in bed. It was a scene that had been repeated countless times before on Sunday nights. I undressed and got in bed beside her.

I tried to chat a few minutes, but she seemed cold as the weather outside. "What's up?" I asked, putting my hand on hers.

"Nothing," she said, pulling her hand away.

"Nothing? You're sure? You're acting a little funny for nothing to be wrong."

"No—nothing's wrong," she answered stiffly.

"Well, it sure seems like it to me," I said softly.

She sat up abruptly in bed, tears brimming in her eyes, her pretty face twisted. "You pay attention to everybody but me," she exploded. "Don't I deserve any attention too? After all, I am your wife—you know!"

I couldn't believe my ears as I looked at Wanda, now crying uncontrollably. Our home and family life had always been so harmonious. With one exception, the time Johnny ran away from home for a couple of days back in 1967, our home life had been tranquil. I was the typical aggressive preacher with four or five major projects booming at the same time. Wanda was the dutiful wife. That's the way it had been when I was in the Baptist ministry. And it was just carried over in the charismatic realm.

I took her into my arms. "Yes, honey, you know you count too. I love you. You've made this ministry a success. Without you backing me up on the homefront, I wouldn't be able to do half of what I'm doing."

"Oh, you don't mean that," she sobbed. "If you did, you'd pay me more attention."

"Honey, I'm sorry," I responded, fully meaning what I said. "I've been so busy with the school and the church. I know you deserve more attention. I promise—if you'll forgive me—we'll work it out. I'll take more time off for us and the kids."

Wanda slowly calmed down accepting my apology and forgiving me. I knew she had been right but I felt under such a strain.

That was just typical of pressure I was under. People were always making demands on my time and for some reason, I always tried to respond. Now I had problems on the homefront. Even there I had to make changes.

As the charismatic movement grew in numbers, people continually visited in Pensacola. "I wish we had a church like this back home," they always remarked. "I sure wish you could help us."

I didn't actually know how I could help those people. I was only one man and there was just so many hours in a day. I was continually getting calls for ministry in places where I couldn't spare the time. In the future, I hoped many of the young preachers graduating from Liberty would fill these needs.

Then in the spring of 1970, I was speaking before a regional meeting of the Full Gospel Business Men's Fellowship in Jackson, Mississippi. One night as I stood before the gathering to teach, the Holy Ghost came down upon me.

As I looked out over more than a thousand faces in the auditorium, I began to weep. The thoughts pressed in upon me—"Most of these people have no where to go to church, no place where they can be fed spiritually." I wept.

A holy hush moved over the people as a prophetic word from the Lord rose up within me. "Thus saith God, I shall raise up pastors to care for and minister to My people. I shall not leave them without comfort. I am not a shepherd who does not care for the sheep of His pasture. I care for My sheep. And I declare before heaven and earth that I will raise up from across the length and breadth of the land pastors to care for My people."

There was a deep moving of the Spirit among the people that night. Many wept too. But more than that, the prophecy also shaped my role. I felt a stronger burden to disciple young men and women. In a first-hand way, I saw how it had affected people like Ralph Lee. And I became burdened to train young pastors to respond to this need.

Both the church and the college were growing by leaps and bounds. By 1972, over 150 students were enrolled in the school. The college's development was beyond my fondest dreams.

Most of the kids were singles so the school had to provide a place for them to live. At first, we purchased several houses around the church property on 57th Avenue. Then, when numbers increased, we bought a large house in the downtown historical district of Pensacola.

Even though the school's housing situation was adequate, it wasn't the most desirable arrangement. Being in a residential neighborhood, people were already complaining about the number of students living around the church. I knew we'd ultimately have to move.

It was during this time that we began praying about the situation. Bob Bishop and Bill Caffey had both become full-time staff members by this time and we realized we needed some property where all the buildings could be arranged in a campus-like setting.

Bill Pace, a vice president with Barnett Bank, had been in our church for a couple of years. I mentioned to him one day the possibility of looking for some land for the church. I knew he had information on various parcels of property around Pensacola.

Within a few days, Bill called for an appointment. That afternoon he met Bob Bishop and myself with a handful of papers. "You'll never believe what I've found in reviewing some papers in our trust department," he hinted, a sly grin beginning to break over his face.

"What's that?" I asked.

"I've found a stretch of land along Highway 98 that may be just exactly what you're looking for," he announced.

"Highway 98, huh? That's good property," Bob commented.

"Yeah, it is," he agreed. "This tract is about eighty acres total that has been reduced to about seventy-five because of highway right-of-ways. The woman who owns the property lives in Chicago. All I need to do is get your okay to talk with her."

"Well, if that's all you're waiting on," I laughed, "then go to it."

Several weeks passed before I heard from Bill again. Then one day, he telephoned. "Brother Ken, that property situation on Highway 98 has gotten a little more entangled since I last talked with you," he reported.

"Oh, what's the trouble?" I asked.

"Well, it seems as if the woman in Chicago doesn't quite own the property entirely. Five other relatives are also involved even though the woman in Chicago has paid the property tax since 1932. If we can't work out a settlement with those people, I think this case might wind up in court—it's just that serious."

"Wow! Sounds a little hot, doesn't it?"

"Sure does," he agreed.

And sure enough, that's exactly what happened. The five relatives wouldn't allow the Chicago woman to sell the property even though they didn't have enough money to pay her the back taxes. In the end, she took the matter to court.

As the situation unfolded, I began to feel that God was supernaturally setting up a chain-of-events to give the property to Liberty.

During the summer convention of 1972, an annual affair at Liberty, I gathered twenty-five men together and we marched around the property claiming it according to the promise of

Joshua 1:3 "Every place that the sole of your feet shall treat upon, that have I given you..."

That muggy June day when we trooped acros the property amid the dense undergrowth of vines, scrub oak, myrtle and pine trees, I had a special feeling. An inner knowing that this land belonged to us.

The court finally decreed that the property would have to be auctioned off at the courthouse steps. October 2nd, the morning of the bidding, we gathered our best prayer warriors in the church auditorium to pray while the auction was underway. We needed the best we had for the bidding.

Rollin Davis, our attorney, had been instructed to bid a hundred dollars higher than each bid offered. We felt that was the wisest way to approach the bidding, which we realized could go sky-high.

Bidding started at $45,000 but slowly inched up—$50,000; $52,500; $55,000; $57,750; $60,000; then $65,000.

"$65,100!" said Davis, looking around.

Nobody else—from the other five or six bidders—seemed interested in bidding any higher.

"Going once ... going twice ... going three times ... sold for $65,100," announced the auctioneer.

We had the property!

Now all we had to do was raise the $65,100. We had entered the whole venture in faith believing if God wanted us to have the property He would handle all the arrangements. A small binder held the property transaction. Thirty days later our attorney handed over a certified check for the total amount. The people of Liberty had responded to the call for the new property.

Many contractors had thought the property couldn't hold buildings, since it was located in a low-lying, marshy area. As a result only six other bidders had actually participated in the auction. I knew the property would hold buildings since Bill Pace had already flown a specialist to the site from Tallahassee to examine the land. God knew what He was doing in leading us to the spot—the promised land.

However, since the land was low and swampy, it was necessary to dig up the ground from four to eight feet in places and put clay down before any roads or buildings were built. Two men in the fellowship, Larry Bartell and Harry Hegwood, worked for a prominent architectural firm. Feeling this was a natural place to get our work done, we hired their company.

The architects laid out the entire project including almost every conceivable long range possibility. The facilities included faculty housing, eight college dorms, a 1500-seat auditorium, a retirement center, an orphans' home, classrooms. The entire campus would have all underground lighting, telephone lines and wiring. There'd be no utility poles on campus, none to mar the place's natural beauty.

None of us had any idea of all the endless details that went into the planning of a college campus together with the new church facilities. The endless red tape, the contractors, the sub-contractors, the permits, the building codes. It was all eye-opening for the two people coordinating things—me, a country boy from Mississippi, and Bob Bishop, a former Quaker Oats salesman.

When our committee of trustees met for the first time to discuss the building project, I knew a guy by the name of Ed Johns, who had served as a steward with me at Richards Memorial Church. He had been in construction work for years. I wondered if he might be interested in directing the project for us.

"I ain't foolin' around with a bunch of committees," Ed announced in his familiar crusty manner, when he came to meet with the group. "I've done that before. Most of 'em are pretty miserable to deal with."

Smiles crossed everybody's face but Ed's and laughter cascaded around the room as people remembered experiences in other church situations where most every job was attempted through a committee.

"You don't have to worry about a committee," I assured Ed. "All you have to do is work with me and Bob Bishop. The elders will endorse this arrangement, I'm sure."

That seemed to satisfy Ed and he signed on as overall foreman to direct the construction project. I figured we'd be able to move onto the property for anywhere from seven hundred thousand to a million dollars in cost. I must have been dreaming!

God never showed me all the money that was going to be needed or the problems I'd be facing. If He had, I might have backed out completely. I had no earthly idea what was ahead.

FOURTEEN
'73—The Crisis Year

The buildings were beginning to take some crude shape out on Highway 98 around the middle of 1973, but we had problems—unending problems. It rained continually, creating untold delays. The recesssion hit causing bank interest rates to skyrocket along with building costs. And as usual, that caused financial problems for us. Funds were spent practically before they ever hit our checking account. It seemed as if the building project literally swallowed the money like a hungry dinosaur devouring an appetizing meal.

But those were only the most visible problems. There were many others underneath the surface working their way upwards. They all became part of the twelve months known as my crisis year.

It all began in late January. I was in Williamsburg, Virginia leading a Full Gospel Business Men's seminar on healing. Since I hadn't been physically ill in nine years, I figured I was certainly qualified to teach the seminar. In the time since I had received the Baptism in the Holy Spirit, illness had become an unknown thing in the Sumrall household. We had learned to rely on God.

But no sooner had I arrived in Virginia than I got sick. In fact I got so sick, feverish and nauseated that I stayed in bed all day long. At night, I ventured out to the meetings praying for sick people and watching them get healed. Returning to the room, the fever and nausea once again pounced back on me. Unexplainably, that lasted for three days.

Returning home, I was on a plane from Atlanta to Pensacola. Sleepiness had overcome most passengers as the flight roared southward amid a tranquil atmosphere created by the jet engine roar. Heads nodded. Talk ceased. I leaned back in my seat trying to relax.

Out of the corner of my eye, I noticed a middle-age woman in a blue dress across the aisle. She was crying. Her mascara was getting smudged as she dabbed at her eyes with a kleenex. Since the seat beside her was vacant, I crossed the aisle and sat down.

"I noticed you were crying and I'm a preacher," I said softly. "Can I do anything to help you?"

"Oh, thank you so much," she answered tearfully. "I'd like to talk to somebody."

"Well, what seems to be bothering you?"

"It's my sister," she said, still wiping her eyes. "I just got word yesterday that she has a brain tumor. The operation's today and I'm on my way to be with her. They don't expect her to come out of surgery alive. If she does, she'll just be a vegetable."

"Do you believe in prayer?" I questioned.

"On, yes," she said, nodding her head.

"Well, I do too," I replied. "Let's join hands and we'll just pray for your sister right now. What's your sister's name?"

"Lucy Turner."

"You don't mean the Lucy Turner who attends Liberty Church?" I said in astonishment.

"Why, yes. That's her."

"Well, I'm Ken Sumrall, her pastor."

Knowing the person involved, I prayed all the more fervently. Betty, Lucy's sister, seem to grow relaxed after we prayed and I returned to my seat pondering the situation. What a turn of events. I had seen Lucy only a week before. She was the picture of health then.

As soon as the plane landed, I telephoned Wanda that I'd be late coming home and then drove quickly to the hospital. Lucy's surgery had been completed. She was now in the intensive care unit.

Identifying myself as her pastor, I asked permission to pray over her. One of her surgeons was at the desk filling out a chart when I entered the room. "I guess it won't hurt now," he said, looking grim. "We've done everything we can do, but she's just about gone."

Lucy's head had obviously been shaved for the operation. Bandages were wrapped thickly around her skull. Her skin was ashen and cold. Life support machines hummed. I stayed for several hours praying and rebuking death.

For several hours Lucy's fate hung between life and death, then unexplainably she took a turn for the worse. Death came swiftly.

The funeral was scheduled at Liberty the following Monday. The day before I was in my office getting prepared for the morning service when a knock came. It was Shirley Dexter, a tall burnt-brown woman with hair and eyes lighter than her skin.

"Brother Ken, I have a word from the Lord about Lucy," she announced, closing the door behind her.

"What is it?" I asked, motioning her to have a seat.

"We're supposed to raise her from the dead," she responded.

"Who's included in the we?" I questioned.

"Well, four other ladies and myself feel like God has told us we can raise her from the dead."

"Praise the Lord," I said.

"That's not all God said," she volunteered.

"What else did He say?" I asked, anxious to hear.

"He said the way to do it was after you get through preaching tomorrow you're to turn the service over to us. We're going to come up to the casket and command her to rise. A lot of people will be saved as a result of this."

"I don't witness to this at all," I said kindly. "I get a witness it's the enemy trying to embarrass us."

"Why?" she asked, surprised at my response.

"I read recently this was attempted in San Diego when a group decided they were going to raise somebody from the dead and they called the newspapers. I saw the news account in a fundamentalist magazine. They tried to discredit the charismatics with the foolishness of the act. They didn't raise the person in San Diego and to be honest with you, I don't think you folks will either. But if you want to try, you can raise her anytime before ten o'clock Monday morning. After that time, I'll take the service and I can't give it to you."

She reacted harshly. "Well, you're going to be responsible if she's not raised from the dead," she threatened, her eyes flashing.

"I'll just have to take that responsibility unless the Lord shows me differently," I replied.

As soon as Shirley left, I went out, located two of the church's pastors and explained the story I had just been told. They were skeptical too. I walked back into my office and prayed more about the situation. As I did, the Lord impressed me that before He ever raised anybody from the dead He had healed the lame, the blind and all kinds of other sicknesses.

With that bit of information in my spirit, I stepped out into the sanctuary looking for Shirley. I found her sitting with her husband, a commander in the Navy. "Can I see you a minute?" I asked, trying to get her out of earshot of her unsaved husband.

"The Lord has impressed me before He ever raised anybody from the dead He had healed all kinds of people," I said, as we walked to the back of the building. Her eyes widened. "We have some palsy cases who regularly sit near the front of the auditorium and this morning at the altar call you can get those four ladies together. If you raise one palsy case, you can take the service tomorrow."

"That's not what the Lord told me," she shot back.

"I'm sorry, that's what He's saying to me," I responded firmly. "And that's the way, it has to be."

The next day I conducted the funeral and Lucy was buried. The five women didn't attempt anything that particular day. What I didn't realize, however, was they had begun a program against me. They began praying—asking God to break Ken Sumrall!

All through the summer months, it rained abnormally heavy. It seemed as if the rain fell day and night. Construction lagged. The county engineer, whose job was in limbo with the county commission, caused enormous problems by requiring us to obtain a new permit every time we made a construction change. New drainage codes were being enforced rigidly. Several times work had to be stopped because of the permit situation. A county commissioner, Zearl Lancaster, intervened on our behalf once when the situation was at its worst.

Then, there was the ever-present problem of money. We had raised the $65,100 for the property purchase as well as another hundred thousand just to get construction going. But money was ever slowing in coming. I had never seen the likes of such a struggle. At times, it seemed as if we could hardly get a prayer through. Many times I called the church to prayer and fasting. It seemed the devil was there to kick us every door we walked through.

In July, I was in Charleston, South Carolina speaking to a Full Gospel Business Men's meeting. Afterwards Wanda and I drove to Greenville to visit with my brother. We later went over to Airport Baptist Church where I had pastored many years before.

Pulling onto the church parking lot, I noticed the car went up in front and down in back—producing a slight jarring motion and making a scraping sound. Not realizing some wiring for a trailer hitch had scraped the pavement also, I didn't recognize the seriousness of the problem and drove across the parking lot to where a man was mowing grass near the building.

I identified myself and chatted with the man for awhile. All of a sudden, I noticed smoke drifting from under the hood of the car. "I didn't know the car was that hot," I remarked.

"I reckon it is," he agreed.

In a few minutes I looked up and the smoke was still curling up looking heavier all the time. "I'd better check this out," I said, running over to the car.

I hurriedly hit the hood latch and yanked the hood upwards. Billows of smoke poured from the engine. Seeing an electrical wire smoldering, I grabbed and threw it to the ground. Immediately as I seized the wire, I knew I'd made a mistake. It was red hot.

"Ken!" Wanda shouted, looking at my right hand.

Then, I looked. The flesh on three of my fingers was seared to the bone. A fourth was also branded. "I've burned my hand," I said. As I spoke, I could feel the hand beginning to throb painfully.

"We've got to find a doctor," Wanda said.

Even though we got lost several times in Greenville, the pain had just about stoped by the time we found a hospital. Both Wanda and I had prayed fervently over the hand. Hospital technicians rushed me into an emergency room and dunked my hand into cold water laced with ice. Then, a doctor walked in to examine the hand.

"I'll have to keep you here a couple of days," he announced, pouring a cleansing solution over the wound.

I shook my head. "I can't do that," I responded. "I'm due to preach in Hickory, North Carolina in a seminar tomorrow."

"Man, you can't go off with a hand like that."

I smiled. "You dress it, doc, and leave it to me," I replied.

The doctor continued trying to talk me out of leaving as he dressed my hand. But I wasn't about to stay in the hospital. The next day I preached in Houston Miles' church in Spartanburg. I was even clapping my bandaged hand and didn't feel a thing. I went on to Hickory, preached the seminar, and never felt another pain. The burns healed rapidly without any further problem.

Still I had not yet begun adding up the problems facing me.

The next month I was in Birmingham, Alabama involved in a teaching seminar. One night while illustrating the story of how Bob Buess ran across the platform at me resulting in the Sumralls getting a new house, I tripped on the microphone cord and fell. My back struck the podium as I tumbled over.

The audience sat back in amazement at first. They didn't know what to make of my antics. Some thought I was simply clowning. Finally, I crawled to my feet with several men's help and struggled to get my breath. Through blood and guts, I finished the teaching session—in great pain.

I returned to Pensacola but I was sick, deathly ill. I had decided I was going to tough it out and believe God for my healing. But the pain in my chest grew stronger. Breathing was difficult.

One morning, the pressure became so unbearable I called Charles Freeman, one of our pastors, to my house and asked him to pray for me. Relief didn't come though and I called two more pastors, Bob Bishop and Bill Caffey, to join in the prayers. Still the pressure in my chest was excruciating.

"Ken, I think you ought to see a chiropractor," Caffey finally suggested. "You probably need a spinal adjustment."

The three men left and Wanda helped me dress. We drove to the chiropractor's office and walked into a busy waiting room. I became nauseated, went to the restroom and passed blood. When I walked back into the waiting room, Wanda was talking with the chiropractor.

"Man, you're yellow as gold," he said in a startled tone. "You've probably punctured your liver and you've got traumatic hepatitis which is fatal."

"I reject that," Wanda and I both chorused at his diagnosis.

Not being charismatic, the doctor didn't understand our actions. "I can't treat you for this," he said tersely. "You need to get over to Baptist Hospital and let them x-ray for this."

Wanda and I took his suggestion and drove to the hospital. All the while, the pain grew more intense.

Dr. Kennedy, my regular physician, came in and gave instructions for the x-rays. The technicians were back in a few minutes with what looked like a black negative. "There's something covering his chest cavity," one of them suggested to Dr. Kennedy.

"Hmmmmm," the doctor pondered.

In a few minutes, Dr. Kennedy injected a long needle in my chest cavity and came back with a syringe filled with blood. In all he drew a quart of blood out of me. "I'll have to admit you to the hospital, Ken," he said somberly, "You've got some problems."

"Oh, no," I groaned.

Another series of x-rays revealed the source of the problem. I had five broken ribs—obviously from the fall in Birmingham. "The pain you've been experiencing is coming from blood filling up your chest cavity and from the five broken ribs," explained Dr. Kennedy.

"What can be done about it?" I asked.

"The only thing is to use a hypodermic needle to remove the blood and keep the ribs strapped," he answered. "We'll have to draw the blood often as it fills up your chest cavity. If we don't, it could be fatal. We'll also feed you vitamin K to clot the blood."

After the first week in the hospital, I improved greatly. The pain in my chest had practically vanished due to the "blood lettings." I had already cancelled one meeting at the Tennessee Georgia Camps because of the accident and I had another one on the schedule at Jackson, Mississippi. Not wanting to cancel another meeting, I convinced Dr. Kennedy to release me from the hospital.

During the middle of the seminar in Jackson, the chest pains came back. I finished the teaching session the next day and got one of our men to drive me home. I went back to see Dr. Kennedy first thing. As usual, he had me x-rayed.

"You're filled up with blood again," he said. "We need to put you back in the hospital."

"No, doc," I pleaded, "just drain me in your office."

Dr. Kennedy was reluctant but he finally gave in.

But two days later, I was back in his office. Once again, he had me x-rayed. "You're full of blood again," he said. "You haven't quit bleeding yet."

"Can you do it here in your office?" I asked sheepishly.

"No sir," he said firmly, "and I'm not going to treat you any-more unless you submit to me and do exactly what I tell you."

I knew Dr. Kennedy meant what he said. "Okay, doc, I submit to you," I agreed.

"You're not going to get out of the hospital until I tell you. Right?"

"That's right," I mumbled.

Once again, I went back to the hospital and was admitted. The following day, Dr. Kennedy planned to do the "blood letting" in the operating room. "We'll be able to take better care of you that way," he suggested.

That day, the church went to prayer and fasting for me. People recognized that my problem was a lot more serious that had been first thought. Not only did other folks get serious about my condition, I got serious too. We all bombarded heaven for my healing!

Early in the morning, a nurse came into my room and gave me a shot. In a few minutes, I was sick. By the time I was wheeled into the operating room, I was heaving. Dr. Kennedy examined me closely.

"I think we'll just let Ken sleep today," he said finally. "We'll watch him real close and we'll do this in the morning. He's not full of blood right now and I believe he's out of immediate danger."

The following day, the same procedure was repeated. A nurse came in and gave me a shot. But once I was placed on the operating table, Dr. Kennedy couldn't find any blood. He turned me in every direction but he couldn't locate any blood in my chest cavity.

"Let's take him back for x-rays," he suggested, "and see what's the matter."

After the x-rays, I was taken back to my room. Dr. Kennedy walked in a short time later. "According to the x-rays, there's no blood in your chest cavity and your ribs look okay too," he announced.

"Praise the Lord," I shouted.

"I'd like to check you over further," he said, proceeding to run his stethoscope over my chest. After a few minutes, he pulled his instrument from his ears. "You're just as normal as if you'd never had an accident," he pronounced, looking slightly bewildered.

"Hallelujah," I enthused.

He smiled broadly. "I tell you what," he grinned. "I'd let you go home if I didn't think you'd be preaching Sunday. But I'm not going to release you until Monday. You can stay right here in the hospital until then. That way I know you'll be resting."

A number of the college students came that afternoon to sing and praise the Lord with me. Then, Beth Bishop walked in. "Bob's sick in bed," she explained, "that's why I brought this note."

I looked at Bob's scribbled note. "Ken, we have been turned down by the bank for the $125,000 loan we need. If we don't get the money from some source, construction on the buildings will have to stop. Bob."

The word source seemed to reach off the paper at me. "Source," I thought to myself. "God is our Source. He's in this project with us. I know He is."

Beth looked at my face trying to read my reaction. "What do you think?" she questioned.

"It's good news," I answered. "Bob says we've been turned down for a bank loan. It looks like we'll have to truly rely on God now. Hallelujah! God's already done one miracle today. I'll start believing for a second right now."

"Careful," she cautioned. "You're not supposed to get agitated."

"That's all right. I think God is going to do something big. Tell Bob that. See if that doesn't make him feel better."

And that's what happened. We applied at another bank for the same kind of loan and got $250,000—double the amount we had been turned down at the first bank. It was more than enough money to get the project on the right track.

Several times the Lord supplied $20,000 and $25,000 from people—some even from folks who normally would have cared nothing about Liberty's building project.

It seemed as if we had just passed that financial crisis when another one—just as dark—struck. Shirley Dexter walked into my office again. "I have a word for you," she announced.

"What is it?" I questioned, wondering what she had come up with now.

"You're going to die!"

"Well, if you're trying to get my attention, you've got it," I said. "When am I doing to die?"

"Real soon."

"Did the Lord tell you why I'm going to die?" I asked.

"Yeah. He said to tell you to read Ezekiel 33 and 34."

I sat back in my chair and thought for a moment. "Well, Ezekiel 33 speaks about the judgment of God on Israel and the prophet of God being God's watchman. Unless he told them God's judgment was coming, their blood would be on his hands. Are you saying you're a spokesman for God to tell me God's going to judge me and if you don't do it, the blood is on your hands?"

She sat quiet, not responding to my words.

"Ezekiel 34 talks about false shepherds," I continued. "Is that what you're saying I am?"

"I'm not saying anything," she replied, seeming pleased with herself. "God just said to tell you to read Ezekiel 33 and 34."

"Okay, I'll read them," I promised.

And I proceeded to read the chapters—getting under condemnation as I did. Everybody can think of a few things that God probably ought to kill him over. After I'd severely burned my hand and broken five ribs, I was beginning to wonder if there wasn't a possibility to what the woman suggested. Later, I called a pastors' meeting and told the men it had been prophesied over me that I was a false shepherd.

"Aw, Brother Ken, there's nothing to that," Bob Bishop suggested. "Don't listen to that stuff."

I drove home from the meeting and told my wife what had happened. She tried unsuccessfully to cheer me up. The more I thought about it—with all the problems I'd faced that year—maybe God was going to kill me.

Several days later, I went to Dothan, Alabama for a seminar. I was heavily burdened and spent most every night in prayer. Early one morning after I had walked the floor, praying and crying all night long, God spoke.

"I didn't make that woman a watchman over you," He declared. "She's a false prophetess and you're going to have to break this power from your church."

Iron fetters seem to lift off my spirit as I heard those words. Chains seem to break from around me. "Glory! Praise the Lord!" I shouted. Joy bubbled up within me. I knew I had heard from God.

After teaching that morning in the seminar, I drove back to Pensacola to preach the evening service at Liberty. On the way, God gave me a message on "Be Not Deceived." The Scripture text was taken from Matthew 24. My first point was "All sinners are deceived." Secondly, "Some Christians can be deceived." Third, "Some of us are." Then, I related the story of what had happened to me during the year.

"There are five ladies sitting out here tonight that are practicing witchcraft," I told the congregation. "You're members of this church. One of you told Brother Freeman several weeks ago to get ready to take over this church because I was going to die. Obviously you missed God. All of the prophesying over my life trying to control me is over. Finished. And all of your witchcraft influence of this church is over."

Though I was speaking strongly, I felt completely confident that I was giving God's message for the hour. My heart burned within me.

"Here is the way this is going to be handled," I announced. "Tonight if you come to this altar and tell me you're repenting, then I'm not going to call your names publicly. The second choice is that you can go out the back door and never come back here again—never!"

I had never heard such a large auditorium get so quiet. People were deeply moved. They knew God was speaking through me.

"Let's stand and sing. Folks, let God have His way in this altar call. You come for prayer. Get your needs met. Let's sing."

Instead of inhibiting the altar call, my words spurred it. People flooded toward the front. Four of the five women also came forward. Shirley vanished out of the back door and into the night. It was the last I saw of her.

For weeks I felt great. Nothing seemed to bother me. The air had cleared. Growth continued at both the church and college. Construction work hummed along steadily.

Yet as quickly as it had gone, the pressure came back. The need for finances always seemed to be with us. The recession had struck with devastating power. It seemed as if we didn't have an extra dime left for anything. Construction costs ate every cent we raised.

One Sunday morning the burden was so overpowering I got another pastor to preach for me and I drove to the building site. Buildings were in various stages of development. Some were almost complete. Others, hardly started.

"This year has been such a struggle," I thought to myself. "Will we ever get in these buildings?"

I didn't have any answers. I wondered if the building program would ultimately fall through. Would the buildings remain just like some unfinished giant—hollow and empty? I had no way of knowing.

For the next two hours, I walked over the property praying and talking to God. Then, Jerry Webb and Bob Bishop drove up. Jerry was handling the electrical end of the construction, but he too was sorely pressed for funds. He had put a lot of money into missions and into the church. Now he—like Liberty—needed to hear from God.

A number of expensive construction items would soon be delivered. Funds would also be needed to pay for them. "I don't know, Ken," Jerry remarked about the materials. "It looks real bad."

Bob seemed non-committal.

Then, it suddenly struck me. "Aw, praise God, fellows," I shouted. "If we go broke, let's go broke big and carry God down with us. God's the one who led us into this thing. He's responsible for it. If it's of God, it'll go. And if it's not, we ought to know it now."

"That's right," Bob agreed. "Let's just let the material come in and we'll just conduct ourselves like we have all the money we need."

That same spark of faith had ignited Jerry too. "Amen," he enthused. "Let's find out how big God is."

In short order, I figured we'd know the answers. And we did. People were soon coming out of the woodwork with money for Liberty. I knew it was God. He alone knew the need. He alone could work such a miracle.

Groundbreaking for the present Liberty Church facilities.

Construction gets underway for Liberty Church and Liberty Bible College, 1973.

FIFTEEN

"They'll Buy It . . . They Can't Help It!"

Even though some of the more pressing financial problems were being solved, getting moved to the new campus was becoming a greater dilemma every day. It seemed like every time we set a date for moving we were unable to follow through. Roadblocks and obstacles abounded.

Finally I announced in desperation, "We'll be on the new property next Sunday—so don't come here. Go to the new place."

I believed we would be on the new property whether or not the buildings were ready. We had done that during the early days on 57th Avenue. We could do it again now.

But there were plenty of problems facing us. One problem in particular. I had been trying to sell the property on 57th Avenue for over six months. In fact, I had written letters to every church and pastor in town. But nobody responded.

Then one day I was driving into town thinking about the problem when the words "school board" came to mind. Even though I couldn't imagine the school board wanting a church building, I drove down to their main office. I didn't want to miss an opportunity especially if this was God's leading.

Dr. Roger Mott, Assistant Superintendent of Schools, was an old acquaintance. "Roger, you may think I'm a little foolish, but I came by to tell you I've got a church building for sale. If you're in the market for a building, it's available."

A tall, dark and imposing man, Roger looked surprised.

"That's odd," he said, shifting in his swivel chair, "just last night at a board meeting we decided to buy a building or put one up for about five hundred people to train teachers."

I smiled, thinking about the leading of the Holy Spirit. "Well, that's exactly what ours was built to hold," I enthused, "besides an auditorium we've got a lot of other space."

"Hmmmm, this sounds good," he replied.

Dr. Mott called the superintendent of education and that afternoon they drove out to look over our facilities. They both were thoroughly impressed and promised to report back "as soon as possible."

I just *knew* the property was sold. Any day I expected to get a telephone call reporting everything was finalized. "Come by and get your check," I heard them say in my thoughts.

But the fact of the matter was I didn't hear anything. September arrived and there was still no news. I anxiously telephoned Dr. Mott. "Has anything been settled on the building?" I enquired.

"We're still working on it," he responded. "But I think everything is still pretty safe. These things just take a little time."

I existed on his "little time" words for a while but then two more months passed without any further word. December came. Time was arriving soon for us to be moving to the new facilities. I went back to see Dr. Mott. This meeting was entirely different from the first.

"Ken, I think you'd better just put that property back up for sale," he said, somewhat discouraged. "I don't believe we're going to buy it now. You know how politics are. And this thing looks like it's all caught up in politics for the time being."

What Dr. Mott didn't know was I had already been trying to sell the property—to anybody and everybody. But I had been totally unsuccessful.

I walked out of the school board building disheartened. For months I had been telling people the school board was going to buy the property. Now—they weren't.

"I've wasted six months," I told myself dejectedly.

Cars whizzed down the street. Heat waves rose from the roadway. I looked back at the building wondering what I was going to do now.

"They're going to buy it," the Lord suddenly spoke to me. "They can't help it."

Immediately I started rejoicing. "Praise the Lord," I shouted, getting into my car. "Praise God."

I knew God hadn't let me down. I drove back to the office singing and praising God. Bob Bishop saw me walk in. Seeing my face in smiles and knowing I'd been to the school office, he added two and two together and rushed into my office.

"Well, what'd they say?" he asked excitedly, a wide grin on his face. "Did they say they're going to buy it?"

"No, they didn't say they were," I announced. "In fact, they told me they weren't."

Bob's facial expression changed, growing somber. "Then, what're you all smiles about?" he asked, puzzled at my actions.

"The Lord said they would buy it," I grinned.

"Oh," Bob muttered.

After that, we didn't do another thing about the property— no more advertisements or efforts to sell it. For my part, I simply thanked God every time the situation came to mind. I was standing on God's Word—His expressed will to me. Based on the promise of 1 John 5:14, 15 ("if we ask any thing according to his will . . . we know that we have the petitions that we desire of him"), I knew it couldn't fail.

Two days before we were to move, Dr. Mott telephoned. "We're ready to do business with you, Ken," he announced happily, "if you still have that building."

"Well, praise God," I replied, "I'm ready too, and we've still got it."

Before the week was out, the school board had given us a check for twenty thousand dollars *more* than we had invested in the 57th Avenue property all total. What a miracle!

That was one problem solved, but there were still others to take its place. Thinking that electrical and water connections would be hooked up that last week, we optimistically moved all the dorm students into the two new dormitories.

But we didn't have either water or electricity. The bathrooms couldn't be used, nor could the kitchens. There was no water even for drinking purposes.

Friday morning after two days of being "without", I called the students together for a chapel service. The atmosphere was tense from the few days of hardships. Ed Zipp, a tall, husky student, asked for permission to speak.

A natural comedian, Ed had everybody rolling with laughter in just a few minutes. Likening the students to the children of Israel and myself as Moses, he moaned, "Brother Ken, you've led us out here in this wilderness . . . and now we're going to thirst and starve to death. It'd be better if we were back in Egypt over there on 57th Avenue eating garlic and onions than out here in these sorry facilities. We need a new leader!"

Ed's comedy broke the tension. It was well-needed.

I had been in a struggle with the water company for four months. That's how long I'd been requesting hook-up to the city facilities.

"Don't worry about it," I was told. "It's no problem, just a simple matter of hooking you up to the city pipes."

Two days before we were due to move, the water company showed up. Four of their men had dug a large hole and were down in it when I walked up. "Hi, fellows, I'm Pastor Sumrall. How're you doing?"

One of the men, a short man with a tough-bulldog face, shrugged. "We've got a problem," he announced.

"What's the problem?" I asked.

"We don't have a connecting valve the size of our pipes and yours. We'll have to order one."

My temper got hot. "You're going to do what?" I shot back.

"We're going to order a valve," he repeated.

"No sir, you won't order any valve. You're going to create one if you have to. Your company has put me off for four months. You go tell your boss I mean to have that water out here tomorrow. I don't care how he does it. I don't care if he has to create a valve—just get the water on."

I walked off—hot and mad. As I strolled around the college watching the finishing touches being applied to the buildings, I realized I had acted unkindly to the workmen. I walked back out to where they were.

"Men, the Lord impressed me that I needed to come back and apologize to you because I had acted so ugly. I realize you're not responsible for this problem. God said He'd take care of it if I turned it over to Him. That's been hard on me but I want to apologize to you."

"Yeah, you have been pretty ugly," one of the men remarked.

Almost immediately, I wanted to get defensive but I didn't. "Yeah, I was ugly," I admitted.

I went on about my business and that afternoon the water was turned on. Virtually the same thing happened with our chair situation. We had tried for months without success to get nine hundred chairs for our auditorium. The factory said it was impossible to deliver them by our dedication day. Yet late

Saturday afternoon—just hours before the opening service in the new facility—a large truck pulled up in front with the chairs.

"Thank You, God," I murmured as the truck was unloaded. "You always meet the needs of Your children."

It was a week of highs and lows, mountains and valleys, problems and miracles. One problem after another rose up, only to be overcome by a miracle from God. The hand of the Lord was upon the new facility.

Sunday—March 17, 1974—our first service was held on the property. Since we had planned to construct an auditorium later, we met first in the cafeteria of the activity building. It ideally accommodated the crowds of seven to eight hundred people who were now attending.

The altar sat snug where the new cafeteria serving line was to be. "How perfect," I thought as the service got underway that day. "You can get spiritual food on one day and physical food the next in practically the same location."

It was a memorable day of dedication. Del Storey, our guest speaker, preached with a great anointing. The building was packed, loaded with many visitors from all over the city. It was a time of rejoicing over the mighty deeds God had done.

Prior to our move to the new location, many people didn't even know we existed. God had neatly tucked us away in a residential area of town for over nine years. Now He had brought us out into the light. I knew many exciting days were ahead for Liberty Church.

SIXTEEN

"Help Me Turn This Billy Goat Loose"

Over the years following dedication of the new facilities, the spiritual warfare changed. During the construction, it had been the exercise of faith as the people believed, God provided and the new buildings rose from the old swampland. But then when we moved in "to occupy the land," the shape of the battle changed.

It was still a fight—just as tough and difficult as before—but a battle by anybody's standards. As always I was reminded of the words of Jesus, "from the days of John the Baptist until now the kingdom of heaven suffereth violence, and the violent take it by force" (Matt. 11:12).

Both the school and church grew enormously during this time. Three hundred-fifty students were enrolled in the college. Attendance at church was inching towards the one thousand mark.

Yet in the midst of such spiraling growth, there was a thread of trouble being woven. In time, the thread would wrap around me creating such a web of stress and strain that I wanted to quit—or even die when the problem became so overpowering.

I first noticed the problem in my daily schedule. It seemed like I was always behind in my work—never quite able to catch up. My days were filled from morning to night with appointments and counseling sessions. Then, there was home visitation and the usual weddings and funerals besides preaching twice on Sunday. In addition, I taught in the Bible college and kept a full schedule of outside speaking dates.

It wasn't too difficult to handle a busy schedule when Liberty had been a small congregation of several hundred but as the numbers grew I was sorely pressed physically. I clearly needed some answers for the situation—and quickly.

Then, one night I was reading the Scriptures and came across the account of a smiliar situation Moses faced in Exodus 18. As I read, I saw myself in Moses' shoes. "And the people stood by Moses from the morning unto the evening," I read.

Settling back in my chair, I thought,"Boy, does that ever sound like me."

As I continued reading, I saw an interesting development in the story. God brought Moses' father-in-law along. "The thing that thou doest is not good," he said. "Thou wilt surely wear away, both thou, and this people that is with thee: for this thing is too heavy for thee; thou art not able to perform it thyself alone."

Alone.

The word seemed illuminated on the page. "That's what I'm trying to do. I'm trying to do this thing alone—the old Baptist way." I had been taught the man in the pulpit handled all the chores and that's what I had been practicing. "How do you remedy that?" I wondered.

I read further seeing that Jethro counseled Moses to choose able men to minister to the people and bring the hardest problems to him. "That's it," I shouted, "that's what I need to do. Praise God!"

Hearing my shouts, Wanda strolled into the den. "What's up?" she asked inquisitively.

"Oh, I've just found the solution to my hectic schedule," I beamed.

"Well, anything that gives you more time with your wife and family is okay with me," she announced, taking a seat beside me.

"I think this will do that," I said.

"Good."

In a few days, I shared the idea with Bill Caffey, Bob Bishop and a few others. Everyone agreed the concept sounded perfect. Thus, we launched out beginning a home prayer meeting one Wednesday night a month and also assigning members to certain elders which we chose.

The newcomers didn't seem bothered by the change, but the long-time members were a different story. "Brother Ken, what's the matter?" one man, red-faced and unhappy, cornered me after church. "Don't you want to be my pastor anymore?"

"Sure, I do," I answered, "but my time is so limited. That's why we've appointed elders to look after people personally. We want the church to have more fellowship than just the back of people's heads."

The man frowned. "But we're charter members. We've been with you a long time. All this stuff is okay for the newcomers— but we're different."

"Well, just give it a chance," I suggested, "and try it."

Attendance continued growing and we added a few staff members to help meet the need. We also increased home prayer meetings to two nights a month, then finally we moved to three home meetings a month. One Wednesday night per month, we met in the church for prayer and praise.

I frequently wrestled with strong feelings to be close to the people as in the old days. But I realized the job of ministering personally to such a large congregation could only be handled by a dedicated team of pastors and elders. Reaction to the home meetings and oversight by elders continued to be expressed by a few.

One woman was continually irked. "Brother Ken, you haven't been able to see me in three months. You used to come and see me all the time."

I patted her on the arm. "Now, sister, you know I'll be out to see you one of these days," I responded. "If you've got any problems, just pray about it with your elder."

"No, I don't want to do that," she snapped. "You're my pastor."

"Well, I'll do whatever I can," I said softly, "but I'm only one man. Please just give this change a fair chance."

Many people couldn't seem to understand the demands of being pastor of a church like Liberty. They—like many denominational people—saw the man in the pulpit as their pastor and they wanted personal contact with him or else.

The home prayer meeting/elder concept was only one of the problems. There were other stress-producing matters I constantly faced. One festering problem centered on the subject of discipleship. First introduced into the charismatic movement at a Shepherd's Conference in 1973, the teaching erupted into a public controversy—fueled by hot and heavy rhetoric—in 1975. For several years afterwards, the controversy continued to bubble and ferment.

Two extreme factions arose—those who wanted no oversight but Jesus and those who wanted to be controlled by others to bring maturity to their lives. Liberty Church and myself were caught between the two extremes.

The "freedom" extreme classified us with the "shepherdship heresy" because we were organized into prayer groups with elders. On the other side, we were placed with the "freedom" group by those attempting to pressure us into the strong, exclusive discipleship camp.

A lot of people categorically lumped me into the "shepherdship" group because I had been one of the teachers at the first Shepherd's Conference and also because of my long-time friendship with Charles Simpson, who taught "shepherdship." I always maintained Charles had a perfect right to interpret the Scriptures as he understood them. Yet, that was a prerogative I gave *every* minister of the gospel.

Even in my own preaching and teaching, I had given strong emphasis to submission and headship—perhaps too much emphasis. I agreed that many people attending the large charismatic gatherings were "meeting-hoppers" and "sermon-tasters." I felt that many of them needed to commit themselves to a local fellowship.

Then, because many who were leaving denominational churches were pleading with me to help them establish new charismatic churches in their areas, I chartered Liberty Fellowship of Churches and Ministers for that purpose.

Pastors and congregations began to respond to the new Fellowship. At first, only a few churches in west Florida and south Alabama joined. Then, churches in Mississippi came in.

"Ken, you're going to have to be careful here," Bob Bishop warned one day.

"What do you mean?" I responded.

"You're spreading yourself awfully thin, accepting all these new responsibilities," Bob suggested.

"Maybe so," I answered, "but it's difficult to turn these people away."

Bob nodded his head. "I understand that, but I'm afraid you're letting your heart rule your head."

Within two years, the Fellowship had churches in seven southeastern states. Congregations from as far away as Tennessee were now members.

Since I had been called upon to help start many of these congregations, it was natural for them to look to me for help in their early stages. I had also been "papa" to their pastors when Liberty was much smaller. So, we understandably felt a need to communicate regularly regarding direction for the churches.

In my attempt to build a Fellowship of ministers and churches which would work together in ministry, I made the mistake of setting up a tight "extra local" governmental structure which made certain demands upon the pastors and boxed me into their close supervision. I had taught on apostleship as one of the five-fold ministries (Eph. 4:11) and many looked on me as the apostle in Pensacola. A book I had written, *New Wine Bottles,* also locked me into that role. Before I realized it, the "tail was wagging the dog."

Soon I began to feel the weight of what others had been warning me. Whenever a problem surfaced in the field churches, the people, more often than not, turned to me. If a dispute arose, I had to mediate it. If a pastor had to be replaced, I had to handle it. People expected me to drop whatever I was doing in Pensacola and rush off to put out the fire somewhere else.

Problems leaped out continually in many places where Liberty had churches. The difficulties were always varied, but I consistently found myself in the middle of the situation. In one church, a group of strong-willed trustees attempted to take over the church and fire the pastor. In another, a pastor set business hours for himself and refused to minister to his congregation outside of those hours. In still another location, severe methods of discipleship were applied, creating havoc among the people. Telephone calls and letters frequently arrived from pastors "wanting a word with Brother Ken."

I also placed more demands on myself teaching the "team

concept" of ministry to the graduates of Liberty Bible College. In essence, I was to help build teams on campus which would eventually move to cities in the U.S.A. to begin churches. To begin these teams meant that I had to spend time establishing them on a proper foundation.

"Ken, why do you always let people get you out on a limb?" Bill Caffey questioned once during a staff meeting.

"Amen," Bob Bishop chuckled while I struggled for an answer.

"I'm not sure," I admitted honestly. "It could be an ego problem or just plain concern for these men—maybe a little of both. I know I'm overextended."

Heads nodded around the table.

For somewhile, I willingly or unwillingly allowed the situation to continue—all the while getting more bogged down in the mechanics "greasing the squeaking wheels." I guess I honestly felt a responsibility to the pastors and people that the work of God not be hindered. I wanted to do my part.

Fatigue began to etch itself into my face. I felt tired, listless. My preaching obviously suffered. One day I received an unsigned note. "Brother Ken, what's happened to you? You're losing your anointing."

Bob Bishop noticed the heaviness one morning when we found ourselves alone in the mailroom over a cup of coffee. "Are you okay?" he asked.

"Yeah, sure," I replied.

"You look a little tired," he suggested.

"You're probably right. I haven't been getting much sleep lately. This thing with the Fellowship has just grown beyond anything I ever dreamed. I never knew it would absorb so much of my time."

"I know," he said, "but I think you're simply trying to be too much to too many."

His words bore into me.

"What can I do about it?" I asked, frustrated. "I feel like the kid who grabbed a billy goat by the horns and in a few minutes was yelling, 'somebody come help me turn this billy goat loose'."

A smile creased Bob's face. "You might just have to back off a little," he said softly.

"Maybe so," I answered, walking back to my office.

Many pastors in the Fellowship thought I should resign at Liberty Church in Pensacola and give myself completely to the work in the seven states. Both my sons, Johnny and Stanley, were married now. Beth would soon complete nurse's training and Marlene was out of high school and working. From a family standpoint, I was free to do just that—although I couldn't leave Wanda out of the picture. She had to be considered whatever I did. The past had taught me that.

But the problems with the Liberty Fellowship were only part of my dilemma. On campus, there were troublesome matters as well. A new teacher had worked behind the scenes planting seeds of discontent among students. Two men called a mass meeting of married students to discuss all the wrong things about the college. Many students influenced by shepherdship teaching wanted more personal direction in their lives. Yet because of limited funds, our staff was loaded with work and couldn't give the personal attention many felt they needed.

Then, when it seemed like everything was coming unglued, an undercurrent of criticism surfaced in the church. The church's leadership was criticized for practically every decision it made. A television ministry had been started in 1976 and a few people thought we should eliminate it. Some suggested that we should emphasize ministering to our own people instead of reaching more and more.

"Am I supposed to nail a sign to the door saying 'no visitors'?" I asked repeatedly. I knew we had grown very large but I didn't know how big God wanted us to get.

The pressures bore down heavily—discipleship crisis, troubles on campus, Fellowship problems, criticism in the church. The list seemed to run endlessly. I began to think I ought to respond to the call of the preachers outside of Pensacola.

"Maybe the problem is I'm not obeying God," I thought to myself. "Possibly things will settle down if I just get out."

Frustrated and pressured on every hand, I was nearing an emotional bottom—sunk by the problems. Thoughts of resigning lingered with me for days. Finally, I called a pastors' meeting for the purpose of resigning. The men—Sandy Carson, Bill Stamp, Bob Bishop, Bill Caffey, Don Loose—who had become pastors at Liberty, were people I knew would speak the mind of God to me.

Even though a sense of frustration pervaded the meeting because of the mounting problems, the men had strong feelings about my staying in Pensacola. At the time, my conviction was that God would raise up leadership to replace me if I decided to become a traveling pastor to the Fellowship.

"I feel like you ought to stay here," Bob Bishop said. "There'd be something missing if you weren't here to oversee this place."

"That's right," agreed Bill Stamp. "To consider anything else would be to largely ignore the will of God. You're the man God raised up. I don't see how this group of men could accept your resignation."

In spite of the men's encouragement, I walked out of the meeting disturbed. It was dark that night. No stars or moon were in sight. And that's exactly the way I felt—dark and gloomy.

I went to bed tired and discouraged and woke the next

morning the same way. Wanda was already in the kitchen taking care of breakfast when I crawled out of bed. On my knees, I buried my head in my hands and cried out to God . . . I couldn't go on anymore. This was the end.

"God . . . just a word . . . a word of encouragement . . . something . . . anything . . . God, I'm desperate . . . please . . . ."

Tears drenched my face as I poured out my problem. Then, when the problems seemed to be all wept out, God spoke.

"One of your biggest problems is you're not appreciative of all the good things I'm doing. You have your mind on the negative things which are very few and you're not seeing the hundreds of things that I'm doing that are good. You're just not grateful."

BAM! The words hit me with the force of a ton of bricks.

Almost before my eyes, I could see a picture—like on a motion picture screen—of all the good things God was doing. The 1400 people attending Liberty Church; many getting saved; missionary giving nearing $300,000 annually; the new television studio; hundreds being used in the Bible college.

Then, it struck me. Ninety-five percent of the people were *with* me. It was only a small minority criticizing. God was blessing. We were in His will.

"Oh, God, You're right . . . You're right," I said trembling. I broke and wept before the Lord even more. Healing from the frustration and depression came as I praised God. I was focused on all the negatives and none of the positives. God had to redirect my vision.

My strength came back in record time. Several days later, I confessed my problem openly before the church. That day, God moved with a powerful anointing to set many free.

In time, I called a meeting of the Liberty Fellowship churches. "Men, I think we need to back off a little and let others stretch forth their own faith," I announced. "What has happened in the past hasn't worked very well because it left too much up to one man. We've got to graduate some of these people. It hasn't really been as much of your problem as it has been mine. But now I want our men to stretch forth their own faith for ministry."

Though some of the ministers were uneasy about the change, others said, "I believe we hear you, Brother Ken."

I continued, "I simply need to go from mothering people to fathering them."

The presbytery agreed unanimously. A plan was worked out to redistribute responsibility among six others. I would work with them but they would coordinate the work in their geographical areas.

I had learned some great lessons. These men and churches weren't my responsibilities. They were God's. And if I were an apostle (which was questionable), it wasn't like Paul, who traveled and started churches. It was more like James, who stayed in one place and counseled the brothers from time to time.

As far as the discipleship crisis and criticism of myself and the church, I knew we simply had to continue doing what God had told us. We would make changes only as God gave us understanding of such truth. The prayer groups with elders would continue. We would also continue to maintain that delicate balance between various extremes in the charismatic movement.

Once again in my life, I had to release the pressures and the responsibilities back to God. It was all His business not Ken Sumrall's. What a weight came off me when I discovered that great truth—finally. I didn't have to prop up God's kingdom anymore. He could handle that Himself.

An aerial view of Liberty Church and Liberty Bible College, 1979.

Ken Sumrall and family at Marlene's wedding, 1979.

SEVENTEEN
A New Wave of Glory

In August 1977, some of the women from the church went off to a weekend retreat at a Baptist campgrounds in Alabama. I was due to deliver a brief devotional on Sunday morning. As I drove to the campgrounds, I was praying and singing in the car. It was a sky-blue morning with touches of gold dancing on the few fleecy clouds.

The Spirit of the Lord came over in an unusual way filling the car with His presence. "I am sending a fresh breadth of My Spirit upon the whole charismatic revival and upon you, My servant," He said. "It is a new wave of My Spirit."

The words overflowed me as I heard them. I pulled off the road and praised God freely. Tears ran down. I lifted my hands in praise drinking in the goodness of the Lord and the freshness of His presence.

Needless to say, when I arrived at the campgrounds, I was overflowing with the Spirit. The meeting was fairly routine with a few songs and a prayer or two. Then, it came my turn. The Lord had impressed me to read Psalm 138 and I began reading that heavenly message of praise.

"I will praise thee with my whole heart: before the gods will I sing praise unto thee.

"I will worship toward thy holy temple, and praise thy name for thy lovingkindness and for thy truth: for thou has magnified thy word above all thy name.

"In the day when I cried thou answeredst me, and strengthenedst me with strength in my soul.

"All the kings of the earth shall praise thee, O Lord, when they hear the words of thy mouth.

"Yea, they shall sing in the ways of the Lord: for great is the glory of the Lord.

"Though the Lord be high, yet hath he respect unto the lowly: but the proud he knoweth afar off.

"Though I walk in the midst of trouble, thou wilt revive me: thou shall stretch forth thine hand against the wrath of mine enemies, and thy right hand shall save me.

"The Lord will perfect that which concerneth me: thy mercy, O Lord, endureth for ever: forsake not the works of thine own hands."

I finished the Scripture reading and began praying. As I did, the prayer went from English into unknown tongues. When I stopped and opened my eyes, a holy hush was on the gathering. A woman stood in the back and walked down the aisle with her hands in the air. She was glowing, tears glistened in her eyes.

"The Lord is placing a new breath of His Spirit upon you, His servant," she declared in a trembling voice. "A new wave of God's glory is coming upon you and your greatest ministry is yet to come."

As she finished, the woman toppled to the floor. She was "out" in the Spirit.

The words of Luke 4 and Isaiah 61 were running like a fire through my insides. "The Spirit of the Lord is upon me, because he had anointed me to preach the gospel to the poor; he hath sent me to heal the brokenhearted, to preach deliverance to the captives, and recovering of the sight to the blind, to set at liberty them that are bruised, to preach the acceptable year of the Lord."

I knew it was God speaking.

It had been nearly fourteen years since God thrust me out of the Baptist church and into a new dimension with the Holy Spirit. It had been from one glory to another through the Spirit's leading. The Lord had done so much—healings, miracles, the creation of a Bible college, the beautiful campus and buildings, the missionary outreach. Our television ministry had been invited to be on worldwide satellite. Millions would now hear the Word.

Even though the last fourteen years had witnessed many incredible miracles, I knew something even greater was coming. A new wave of glory was on its way. Not only for Ken Sumrall and Liberty Church but for the entire Body of Christ.

God further confirmed the new wave of glory with the following prophecy which I gave to Liberty Church in October of 1979:

> The time is at hand for a special visitation of the Spirit of God upon you. Heretofore you have tasted of the good things of My Spirit, but compared with the new outpouring the former things will seem as dew and a flood. Sweeping over My people like a glorious tidal wave, all will be effected. Time will be forgotten as meetings will last for hours. Hearts will be melted as My Spirit, like a flame to fire, refines and cleanses. There will be much weeping and sobbing as sin is seen as exceeding sinful and as Calvary love washes them away.

Youth, yes, even the very young, will be drunk with new wine and burn with fervor, oblivious to anything and everything but obedience to Jesus. They too will fall in divine awe before My feet, and former rebellions will be cast away. This flame will spread like a forest fire. Prayer will be the main event of the church. Hundreds will be converted. Be prepared to baptize 200 new believers at one service.

Homes will be renewed and love will flow like a river. Singles will lose their lust for marriage and be knit together in a holy communion. Then My Spirit shall guide them in service for Me. Some will be led to marry, but others will lose all desire for marriage and be wholly Mine to spread the Word they have learned.

Honor My Spirit. Yield to Him. Hear what He says through My proven prophets. New leaders will be needed as a host of new believers will need care. Some leaders who do not respond to My Spirit will be swept aside as I move to lift up a standard against the evil one. For those who hear will come a great refreshing saith the Lord.

Be full of My Spirit and ready to obey Him. I will give a new spirit of discernment to the leaders which will reveal the counterfeit and the fleshly. Walk softly before Me and a holy awe will prevail. The critics will not be able to hinder. Their words shall be swept away before My wave of love and joy. Nor will one man or a few receive glory. I will move upon broken vessels and the fire of My Spirit will break out in homes where My people meet, who seek My face and walk humbly before Me.